Behind the Screen

with Windows 7 and Microsoft Office 2010

by Steve Hayes

Any sufficiently advanced technology is indistinguishable from magic. *Arthur C. Clarke*

First Edition, January 2012

To my wife, partner and best friend Lynne
whose helplessness before the infernal machine
inspired this book

Table of Contents

Preface

- Are you just starting out with a computer that you'll use to write letters, reports and other documents? Maybe you haven't even bought the computer yet.

- Have you been using a computer with a word processor and perhaps a spreadsheet for some time but still find it intimidating and feel that you don't understand what it's doing?

If you fit either description, this book is meant for you. It isn't intended for experienced power-users of a word processor or spreadsheet although they may pick up some useful ideas.

Why this book?

If you've browsed in a bookshop, you'll have seen many vast tomes covering word processors and spreadsheets. This book aims to be different:

- It's much shorter, covering stuff you'll actually use.

- It covers basic skills you need to use your computer as well as how to use the word processor and spreadsheet.

- It leads you through a voyage of discovery: you learn by seeing what needs to be done and then doing it.

- It explains concepts and jargon and tries to give you a mental image of how things work. You'll remember how to do them, see how to do similar tasks and be better placed to figure it out when something you try to do goes wrong.

- It doesn't pretend that things always go as they should.

Because it's very easy to become stymied and dispirited due to a trivial misunderstanding, each chapter works through an exercise step-by-step and early chapters do this in detail with many screenshots. Later chapters assume familiarity with basic operations such as finding something in a dialogue box.

Often there's a choice between doing something the fastest and most efficient way and doing it in a way that's easier to understand and remember. Except for things you'll do often, this book favours the way that's easier to remember.

The exercises are chosen to be as quick and easy as possible to follow while still illustrating concepts, pitfalls and the capabilities of Microsoft Office. Once you're familiar with Office, you'll make documents that are much nicer than the ones produced here.

What word processor?

The book covers use of the Microsoft Word 2010 word processor under Windows 7. Word is part of Microsoft Office.

Microsoft Office costs real money: quite a bit for a version that's licensed for business use. LibreOffice and the very similar OpenOffice are free open-source equivalents and, for most uses, are perfectly adequate. There's a different version of this book which describes how to use LibreOffice. There are two main reasons you might prefer Word:

- It's widely used by businesses and knowing how to use it effectively can be an advantage in the job market.

- Although LibreOffice can save documents in the file format used by Word, there can be minor glitches when these files are opened in Word.

What spreadsheet?

This book covers the Excel spreadsheet which is also part of Microsoft Office 2010.

LibreOffice includes the Calc spreadsheet and much of what's covered here applies to it too.

1 Introduction

1.1 Taking it in

It would be nice if a computer was something like a toaster and a four page instruction leaflet was all that was needed. Unfortunately it isn't like that...

It's not a good idea to read this book all the way through and try to learn everything in each chapter as you go along. You'll get overwhelmed. It's better to work through the exercises, just remembering the bits that seem immediately useful. After you start using them, skim through the chapters again. More of the details will seem relevant.

Perhaps do one chapter a day. You'll remember things better once you've slept on them.

Chapter 2 shows how your computer works and explains a lot of jargon. Chapters 3 and 5 show how to use Windows itself.

Chapter 4 covers the basics of word processing. The concepts and capabilities it describes apply to most word processors.

Chapter 6 covers useful features that even many experienced Word users seem unaware of. Chapters 7 and 8 cover Excel spreadsheets.

Chapters 9 to 11 cover more advanced word processing. You can skim these very quickly just to see what's there, then work through their exercises once you know that the material covered will be useful. If all you want to do is to write the occasional letter, this may be never.

Some versions of Microsoft Office include the Powerpoint presentation program and the Access database. This book doesn't cover those at all.

There is a comprehensive index.

1.2 Conventions

When an important term is introduced, it's shown in **bold**.

From Chapter 3 on, you'll be following through exercises on your computer. In some cases, you need to type in a specific phrase or look for a phrase in a dialogue box or drop-down menu. These are shown in italics, e.g. type *The quick brown fox jumps over the lazy dog.*

> *There are optional paragraphs formatted in italics like this one. They contain information that may be interesting, useful and helps you to understand the steps being described. You can safely skip over them if you want to. Come back and read them later.*

The steps are divided into sections. Each section introduces a few concepts. There's a list of these concepts at the end of the section entitled *What you learned*. Don't worry if you didn't learn all of them – just come back later.

Some of these concepts were only covered in the optional paragraphs. They're shown in italics too. If you skipped the optional paragraphs, you shouldn't worry about these concepts.

2 Behind the screen

*The magical and powerful Wizard of Oz turned out to be
someone very ordinary standing behind a curtain. Computers
may be powerful but they ain't magical.*

"I'm thinking of buying a computer. It has:

- **An Intel Dual Core 3.3GHz processor**
- **4GB of RAM**
- **A 500GB hard drive**
- **An Intel HD2000 Graphics adapter**
- **Windows 7"**

**Sounds impressive but what does it all mean? Once you've read
this chapter, you'll know. You'll also find it easier to understand
why your computer behaves the way that it does.**

Let's start with a machine from the age before computers.

Photo author: Dominic Alves, Brighton, England

This is a teleprinter machine. Like a typewriter, it has a keyboard and a
printing mechanism but it can be connected to another similar machine,
perhaps thousands of miles away. When the operator presses a key on
the keyboard, the corresponding letter is printed on the distant
machine. Before these machines were introduced, messages had to be
sent by skilled operators using Morse code – teleprinters made things
much easier.

On the left hand side of the machine are a roll of paper tape and mechanisms to punch and read it. We'll have a closer look at these because a modern computer uses an electronic equivalent of paper tape to store what you type into it.

When the paper tape punch is switched on and the operator presses a key, a row of holes is punched in the tape and it moves forward one row. A whole message can be saved on tape and stored. At any time, it can be fed back through the reader and the message printed out or sent to a distant teleprinter.

Paper Tape

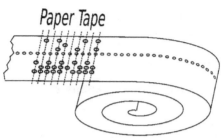

Here's a length of tape with the words *Paper Tape* punched into it. Each letter corresponds to a row of holes in the tape – a coded letter (though not a secret code). The letters *a*, *p* and *e* occur twice and the pattern of holes is the same both times. Also notice that a row was punched when the operator pressed the spacebar between the two words. When the tape is fed through the reader, this row doesn't print anything but, just like when the spacebar is pressed, it causes the printing position to move forward, leaving a blank space.

> *The tape, when bought new, already has the small holes. Each row that is punched can contain up to eight of the larger holes, three on the far side of the small hole and five on the near side. (It happens that the words Paper Tape don't cause any holes to be punched in the nearest position on the tape or in the position just this side of the small holes.)*

You could think about doing some clever things with paper tape.

- You could print the same message many times.
- You could make copies of the tape (the teleprinter itself can do this).
- You could post a copy to someone.
- You could cut up the tape and stick the pieces together to rearrange the words, sentences, etc.

These, of course, are things you can do with a word processor. It does them in much the same way as you could with paper tape, scissors and glue, even using the same codes for the keys pressed, but it does them much more quickly and easily because it keeps the codes in an electronic memory.

2.1 Bits, bytes, characters, numbers and data

At each row on the paper tape, you saw that there can be up to 8 holes. There are 256 (2^8) possible patterns of holes that could be punched in each row (including no holes at all).

Each place that a hole could be represents one binary digit or **bit** of data. If a hole is present, we say it's a binary 1. If it's absent, we say it's a binary zero.

Instead of the presence or absence of a hole, a bit can be represented by an electrical voltage or current – one value represents a zero, a different value represents a 1.

We refer to 8 bits as a **byte** and, as noted above, a byte can have any of 256 possible values. A selection of these can be used to represent various characters – the 26 capital letters (*A-Z*), the 26 lower case ones (*a-z*), the digits *0-9*, the various punctuation symbols, space and other functions such as RETURN (new line). The commonest selection is the ASCII (*American Standards Committee for Information Interchange*) code used by the teleprinter machine above.

Or a byte can represent a number in the range 0 to 255 (or perhaps -128 to +127). Two bytes taken together (16 bits) can represent numbers in the range 0 to 65,535 (0 to 2^{16}-1). Four bytes (32 bits) can represent numbers in the range 0 to 4,294,967,295.

> *Binary numbers of various lengths can be written out (should you ever need to) as a series of ones and zeroes but, if they are long, that quickly gets confusing. It's common to put the bits in groups of four (giving 16 possible values) and represent each group as a number 0-9 or letter A-F. This is hexadecimal notation.*

The term **data** just means information that is stored or transmitted.

2.2 Kilo, Mega, Giga and Tera

In conventional language, **kilo** is 1000, **mega** is 1 million, **giga** is 1000 million (usually called a billion) and **tera** is a million million (1000 billion). For example, a kilometre is 1000 metres.

In some situations with computers (which are pointed out later), different values are used. Kilo can be 2^{10} (1,024), mega can be 2^{20} (1,048,576) and giga can be 2^{30} (1,073,741,824).

2.3 The computer

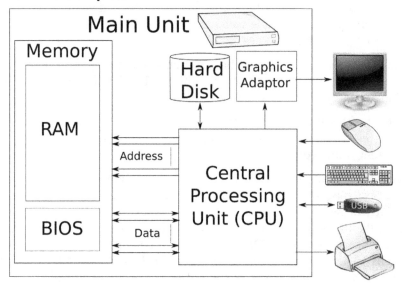

As this diagram shows, the main unit of a typical desktop computer contains (among other things) memory devices, a CPU, a hard disk drive (perhaps more than one) and a graphics adaptor. The memory and CPU are plugged into a large printed circuit board (the **motherboard**). The graphics adaptor may be part of the motherboard or it may be a separate plug-in card.

A display screen (monitor), mouse and keyboard are connected to the main unit. With a laptop, the screen and keyboard are built into the main unit along with, usually, a touchpad in place of the mouse.

The **CPU (Central Processing Unit)** is the heart of the computer. It's a microchip containing complex electronic logic circuits, usually made by Intel (e.g. Pentium) or AMD (e.g. Athlon).

The **memory** is like a huge array of pigeon-holes, each able to hold one byte of data (making each one equivalent to a row on a paper tape).

A number is sent from the CPU to the memory over the address bus to select a particular pigeon-hole. The address bus might consist of 32 separate electrical paths on the mother board – these could select any of 4,294,967,296 pigeon-holes although they may not all exist.

> *Because of the way the addresses work, computer memories have a size which is a power of two. For this reason, their sizes are quoted using the alternative definitions of kilo, mega and giga mentioned previously. For example, a 1 GB (gigabyte) memory can store 1,073,741,824 bytes.*

When the CPU needs to store or retrieve a byte, it uses the address bus to select the required location (pigeon-hole). If it's storing a byte there, it drives the data bus (consisting of eight separate electrical paths) to the voltages representing the byte it wants to store. If it's retrieving a byte, the memory drives the data bus and the CPU looks at the voltages to see what is stored in that pigeon-hole.

> *There's some simplification here. To speed things up, modern computers have 32 or 64 paths in the data bus and can access 4 or 8 successive bytes at the same time.*

2.4 Programs and Data

As you saw, bytes stored in the memory can represent characters or numbers, but they can also represent instructions for the CPU. When the computer first starts up, the CPU reads successive bytes from the memory starting at a fixed location and performs the operations that they specify. For example, an instruction might say to add numbers from two different locations in memory and store the result in a third location. Another instruction might say to compare characters from two locations in memory and, if they match, start fetching instructions from a different location instead of the usual next one.

Although each instruction only specifies a simple operation, a long sequence of them can do something apparently very complex and soph-isticated. A modern computer can carry out billions of instructions every second.

A sequence of instructions makes up a **program**. Your word processor is a program with millions of instructions. Some of them need to be carried out many times over to accomplish even an apparently trivial task such as showing a letter on the screen.

We'll refer to instructions for the CPU stored in the memory as

Programs and everything else (for example, word-processor documents) as **Data**.

When the CPU is following instructions for a program, we say that the program is **running** or **executing** (they mean the same thing).

2.5 Bugs

When a program contains millions of instructions, it inevitably has some logic errors. An error in a program is often referred to as a **bug**. Major bugs are spotted and fixed quite quickly but ones that are only seen intermittently or under unusual circumstances can persist for years before a programmer tracks down what's causing the problem and fixes it.

> *The expression originated when an early computer malfunctioned because of a moth trapped in one of its relays.*

2.6 Crashes and viruses

You're probably wondering how the CPU knows which parts of the memory contain programs and which contain data. The answer is that, in general, it doesn't know. Programs are designed so that, after the CPU processes each instruction, it gets another instruction, not some other piece of data.

Sometimes this goes wrong and the CPU starts treating data as instructions. This rarely causes anything interesting to happen. Sometimes the computer just freezes up. Other times, it detects that there's a problem and either stops the faulty program or stops entirely with an error message (a **crash**). The message may include long numbers in the hexadecimal notation described earlier – only the programmer can make sense of these.

Because of flaws in some of the programs on the computer, malicious people can use various tricks to get it to start running a program that shouldn't be there. This is a computer virus.

> *Strictly speaking, the correct term for all programs like this is **malware**. A virus is malware of a particular type.*

> *An attack often starts when your computer opens something on a page of a dubious website or something attached to a spam e-mail.*

Once an attacker has got one malware program onto a computer, they can use it to install more programs whenever they like. It's common for them to install a program that uses your computer and internet connection to send vast numbers of spam e-mails. They can also use it and thousands like it to overload commercial websites, holding them to ransom.

*A **keylogger** is a very nasty form of malware. It records every key that you press and sends the information over the internet to an attacker. For example, they can see your passwords. That's why most banks require you to click things on the screen to log in – it's much harder to capture that.*

*Attackers mainly target Windows systems although other systems aren't immune. You can buy **anti-virus** programs that try to detect any malware on your computer and block or remove it. Unfortunately anti-virus programs always slow the computer down and some well-known ones can make it intolerably slow.*

A new Windows computer often comes with a trial version of an anti-virus program. Usually, this starts demanding that you subscribe to a paid-for service after 30 days or so.

For home use or in a small business with less than 10 PCs, you can remove the trial program and download and install the free Microsoft Security Essentials from windows.microsoft.com/mse.

2.7 RAM and Hard Disks

Most of the memory in the computer is **RAM**. This stands for Random Access Memory – the name goes back to the earliest computers and isn't particularly meaningful for us. What's significant is that data stored in RAM is lost when the computer shuts down. Copies of programs and important data such as your word-processed documents need to be kept on the **hard disk**. Some people think of the disk as being part of the computer's memory but we'll view it as something separate.

The hard disk contains a number of spinning disks which have a coating similar to that used on recording tapes. Magnetic heads can record data as a series of magnetised regions on the coating, then play them back and recover the data. The magnetised data remains when power is off and the disk can hold much more data than would fit into an affordable amount of RAM. However, the CPU needs to use a program to write data to and fetch it from the hard disk and this is perhaps a million times slower than saving it in and getting it from RAM.

Because the disk is not addressed in the same way as the RAM, 1GB of hard disk space usually means 1,000,000,000 bytes (the conventional meaning of giga) rather than the 1,073,741,824 bytes that 1 GB of RAM could hold.

2.8 The BIOS and booting

Now here's a puzzle. If the CPU needs a special program to get data from the disk and any program in RAM is lost when the computer is shut down, how can it start up again? The answer is the **BIOS** memory. This is a different type of memory known as ROM (Read Only Memory). Data in the ROM is loaded at the factory and is permanent (often a Flash memory is used instead which you can reprogram but that's a complex and risky process). When the computer starts, the CPU begins fetching instructions at a fixed location in the BIOS memory where there's a program that can access the hard disk, copy further programs from it into the RAM and start them. This is the **boot** process – a term inspired by the image of the computer lifting itself by its own bootstraps.

The BIOS allows various options to be set when the computer starts up – you need to hold down a particular key or combination of keys to get to the options. For example, the BIOS can be set to load a program from a DVD or thumbdrive instead of the hard disk when the computer starts. This is the way that programs such as the Windows operating system are installed on (copied to) a new computer.

2.9 Writing a program

This is far beyond the scope of this book but a quick overview might be interesting.

A program as stored on the hard disk or in RAM may make sense to the CPU but it makes no sense to you or me – it's just a series of mean-ingless bytes.

Programs are written in a more user-friendly language using a program quite like a word-processor. The new program (known as **source code**) is translated to instructions understood by the CPU using another program known as a compiler.

Examples of programming languages are Basic, C, C++, C#, Cobol, Fortran, Java, Perl and Python. There are many more, rather more than we really need.

2.10 Operating Systems and Applications

The **operating system** consists of the program that's loaded from the hard disk and started by the BIOS plus a large collection of additional programs that can be started and used to do basic computing tasks such as maintaining data on the hard disk. We'll see some of these programs later on. Examples of operating systems are the various versions of Microsoft Windows, Apple's OS-X and open-source Linux systems such as Ubuntu.

> *Open-source means that the source code of the program is published freely and anyone who wants to can improve it. Open-source programs, including LibreOffice and versions of Linux are normally available at no cost.*

Applications (or **apps**) are programs which aren't part of the operating system itself although sometimes they may be included with it. Most Linux versions automatically include LibreOffice or OpenOffice as a word processor and spreadsheet. Windows includes a very basic word processor – WordPad.

Microsoft Office is an application not included in Windows itself – it must be paid for and installed separately.

> *Smartphones are also little computers with an operating system (e.g. Android – derived from Linux) and apps.*

2.11 Updates

A Windows computer that has an internet connection periodically checks with Microsoft to see if any of its operating system programs can be replaced with newer versions where bugs have been fixed. This is particularly important if the bugs are making the computer vulnerable to malware. If an update is needed, the computer automatically downloads the new programs and installs them. Unfortunately, it usually needs to be restarted afterwards.

Individual application programs may also check to see if they need updating.

Some other operating systems handle updates much better than
Windows.

2.12 The keyboard, mouse and display

Programs running on the CPU need to be able to tell which keys are
pressed on the keyboard and when and where the mouse is moved. We
don't need to examine how this is done.

Programs also need to control the display. The display itself is like a
television – it needs a continuous signal. The Graphics Adaptor creates
this signal. The program only sends instructions to the adapter when it
needs to make changes to the display.

Modern graphics adaptors can be very powerful. This lets the program
create complex images by sending relatively simple and quick instructions to the adaptor. This is a big advantage for game programs but
even the simplest graphics adaptor is sufficient for web browsing and
word processing and other office-type programs.

2.13 The USB thumbdrive and printer

You'll want to connect a printer to your computer so that you can print
out your documents. You may also have a USB thumbdrive / Data
Stick available so that you can save copies of your documents and
move them to a different computer. Even the smallest and cheapest
thumbdrive sold now will be adequate for this.

We can now return to the question at the start of this chapter: what
does all the gobbledegook about that computer mean:

- An Intel Dual Core 3.3GHz processor. This is the CPU microchip. It runs at 3.3 Gigahertz (3,300,000,000 steps per second)
  and has two CPUs internally so it can do two operations simul-
  taneously.

- 4GB of RAM. 4 Gigabytes of RAM can store 4,294,967,296
  bytes, equivalent to nearly 7000 miles of paper tape. It can
  hold many programs and other data at the same time. They
  won't need to be copied to and from the hard disk as often
  which speeds things up.

- A 500GB hard drive. The hard disk could theoretically hold

500,000,000,000 bytes, equivalent to nearly 800,000 miles of paper tape

- An Intel HD2000 Graphics adapter – probably good if you want to play computer games.

- Windows 7 – Microsoft's current version.

This would be a good computer for demanding tasks such as games and video editing. If all you want to do is word processing, spreadsheets, e-mail and web-browsing, any modern computer will be more than adequate and you could save some money.

*In the early days of personal computers, Bill Gates remarked that 640 KB of RAM was all that anyone would ever need. A modern **PC (Personal Computer)** has thousands of times more RAM but Windows still manages to fill it up.*

3 Basics of Windows.

This chapter covers basics such as how to start and close programs, manage their windows and switch between them. Maybe you already know this.

3.1 Clicking and dragging with the mouse or touchpad

When you move the mouse or drag your finger over the touchpad, you'll see a **cursor** move on the screen. This is the **mouse cursor** – it may be an arrow, hand or I-shaped and may change as it moves about. When we talk of **clicking** somewhere or on something, this means moving the cursor to that place on the screen, then pressing the left hand button on the mouse briefly.

Instead of using the left mouse button, you can click with the right hand one. This is **right-clicking** and usually has a different effect from normal clicking.

Clicking the left mouse button twice in quick succession is called **double-clicking**. If you click too slowly, the computer sees your clicks as two normal ones – double clicking has a different effect from this. Sometimes, you need to click three or four times in quick succession: **triple-clicking** or **quadruple-clicking**.

If you keep the left hand button held down and move the cursor, this is called **dragging**. It can be used to move various things around on the screen. They end up in the position that they are when you release the button.

It's possible to change settings on the computer so that the mouse buttons are switched. This may suit left-handed people better. With that setting, clicking and dragging uses the right button and right-clicking uses the left button.

3.2 Starting the Web Browser

Although this book doesn't cover using the web in any depth, it's something you're likely to want to do. This section gets you started but, more importantly, it shows you how to start a program and some of the things to look for in its window.

Click on  at the bottom left of the screen. A box appears on the screen.

*The ⊕ **orb** replaces Windows XP's* `⧉ start`.

This is a **screenshot**. *It's been changed to add candy stripe markings around important things and to blur out irrelevant ones. Section 9.5 shows how you can add screenshots to your documents.*

You'll usually see your choice of web browser program as circled at the top. If this is Microsoft Internet Explorer as shown here, you can just click on it.

Instead, it might be an alternative browser such as Firefox or Chrome. These do the same job but will look a bit different from the screenshot below.

If you want Internet Explorer, click in the Search programs and files box (also circled) and start typing Internet Explorer. As you type, the list of programs above the box changes. Once you see Internet Explorer in the list, click on it.

The computer copies the web browser program from the hard disk into its RAM and starts running it. A **window** appears on the screen.

*In this case, Internet Explorer is showing the Google search page. Google (www.google.com) is the best known and most popular **search engine**.*

Your web browser might start up with a different or blank page. Don't worry.

Near the top left of the Internet Explorer window is a box where you can type the address of a web page. It's circled in the picture above.

Click in the box. All the text in it changes colour – it's highlighted. If this doesn't work, try double or triple-clicking. Type *www.bing.com*. This automatically replaces the highlighted text. Press RETURN (the large key at the right side of the keyboard with a left-facing arrow – it may also say ENTER). The Bing search page loads into Internet Explorer.

Bing is Microsoft's equivalent to Google (even though you're using Windows, you can use any search engine you want). Both Google and Bing search pages feature a box where you can type a question or just some words, then press RETURN. A list of web pages found on the Internet is shown and you can click on any of them to view them. In general, these pages aren't controlled by either Google or Bing: there's no guarantee of their quality, truthfulness or freedom from malware.

If you know the address of a web page, you can just type it directly into the circled box and press RETURN. Further details of using the web are outside the scope of this book.

This book shows the names of keys on the keyboard in capitals. BACKSPACE is usually a large key above RETURN with a left-pointing arrow. The wide SPACEBAR is below the letter keys. ALT is to its left. TAB is near the top left: it may be marked with arrows pointing to left and right. ESC (Escape) should be at the top left. DELETE (or DEL) should be somewhere near the right hand side of the keyboard. There may be CTRL (Control) and SHIFT keys on both sides of the SPACEBAR: you can use the one on either side, whichever is more convenient. The SHIFT keys may only be marked with upward pointing arrows.

*There are also four keys close together near the right-hand side of the keyboard that are marked with arrows pointing up, down, left and right. These are referred to as the **arrow keys**.*

At the top right corner of the window are three buttons (circled). Clicking [X] would close (end) the program – don't click it now.

What you learned:

- **How to start your web browser.**
- **What a window is.**
- **How to go to a web site by typing in its address.**
- *How to find and open a program by typing its name into the Search programs and files box.*
- *Where various keys are on the keyboard.*
- *How to use a search engine such as Google or Bing.*

3.3 Managing program windows

Click on [□] (one of the three circled buttons). The web browser window disappears but, if you look at the **taskbar** at the bottom of the screen, you can see the **icon** for Internet Explorer (e). The browser is still running but has been **minimised**. Thanks to a technique called **multitasking**, other programs can run at the same time – if you want to, you can start another one (e.g. an e-mail program) now. Each program that's running appears on the taskbar and you can switch to it by clicking on its icon.

*When no programs are running or all of them are minimised, most of the screen is occupied by the **desktop**. It may have icons on it: you'll be adding more in Section 5.4.*

If you click on the taskbar icon of a program that isn't minimised but is partly or completely hidden by another window, its window is brought to the front. If its window was at the front, clicking the icon will minimise it. If you can't see the window for your program, try clicking its icon on the taskbar again.

Click 🅔 to restore the web browser window. If the third button is showing a single square (⬜), click on it. The window fills the screen and the button now shows two squares (⧉). This **maximised** the window. You'll usually want the window for your word processor or spreadsheet to be like this so you can see as much as possible of your document unless you're working with another program or document at the same time.

Click on ⧉ . It now shows a single square and the window will prob-ably become smaller.

The markings on the two buttons show what will happen if you click them. The single line looks like a program that's minimised and only visible on the taskbar. The single square looks like a program that's maximised and filling the screen. The two squares represent your program and perhaps another one (or several other programs) visible at the same time.

Place the cursor at the bottom right corner of the Internet Explorer window. It should change to a double-ended arrow. Hold down the left mouse/trackpad button then, keeping it held down, drag the corner so that the window becomes smaller or larger. This is **resizing**: the window stays at the new size when you release the button.

You can place the cursor over any corner or side of the window and, while it's a double-ended arrow, you can drag that corner or side to change the size and shape of the window. Make sure for now that it isn't filling the whole screen.

Now place the cursor over the blank area at the top of the window anywhere to the left of the three buttons. Hold down the left mouse button and move the cursor. The window is dragged. Release the button: the window stays at its new position.

By adjusting the size and position of their windows, you can see and use more than one program at the same time.

The web page may not all fit in the window. If so, **scroll bars** appear at the right hand and bottom of the window. These are marked with arrows in the previous picture. If the window on your computer doesn't have these scroll bars, make it smaller until they appear.

The scroll bar at the right side lets you move the web page up and down in the window by clicking on the arrows at each end, by dragging the large button between them up and down or by clicking on the area below (or above) the large button. Experiment with it.

The scroll bar at the bottom works the same way. It lets you move the web page from side to side in the window.

Other programs including Word and Excel have windows that work the same way as the web browser one. They also have the three buttons and can be dragged and they may have scrollbars.

You can close the Internet Explorer window by clicking on its ▨ X ▨. If you started any other programs, close them the same way. The programs stop running and the RAM they were using is freed.

What you learned:

- **How to minimise a window.**
- **How to maximise a window.**
- **How to resize and move windows.**
- **What scrollbars do and how to use them.**
- **What the taskbar does and where it is.**
- **What an icon is.**
- **How to run more than one program at a time and switch between them.**
- **How to close (stop) a program.**

3.4 Installing Microsoft Office

With luck, Microsoft Office will already be installed on your computer. If it's only a trial version, you'll need to get out your credit card within a month after you start using it and make a payment to Microsoft to unlock it.

A new computer may come with Microsoft Office Starter which has limited capabilities. You won't be able to do the exercises in some chapters until you upgrade it.

You can download Office 2010 from the *office.microsoft.com* website or buy it on a DVD from a computer store where you may get a better price.

Stores sell Product Key versions of Office as well as full versions with a DVD. These are usually slightly cheaper but, while a full version can be moved to another computer (e.g. because the old one broke down), this may not be possible with a Product Key version.

If you have Office 2010 on a DVD or CD, you can install it to your computer by inserting the disk and following the instructions that appear on the screen. You'll probably need to enter an installation key from a sticker in the packaging. Remember that, if the disk is a copy or if it's already been used to install Office on a different computer, you might not be licensed to install another copy on your computer.

Even if Microsoft Office is already installed and unlocked, its version may not be licensed for business use.

Why not avoid all these hassles? You can legally download, install and use LibreOffice instead of Microsoft Office at zero cost. There's a different version of this book that covers installing and using LibreOffice on Windows XP. Use Chapter 5 in this book to learn about Windows 7 instead of XP.

If it's all too complicated, get a friend to sort out your installation. It only needs to be done once.

3.5 Turning the computer off

When you've finished working with the computer you should turn it off correctly so that all documents, settings, etc. are saved.

Click the 🔵 orb, then click [Shut down] at the bottom right of the panel that appears (circled below). After a delay, the computer turns off.

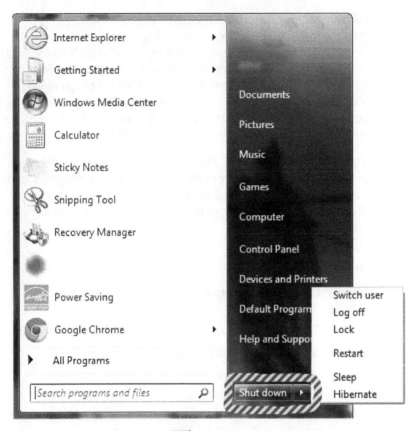

Internet Explorer ▸
Getting Started ▸
Windows Media Center
Calculator
Sticky Notes
Snipping Tool
Recovery Manager

Power Saving
Google Chrome ▸
▸ All Programs

Search programs and files 🔍

Documents
Pictures
Music
Games
Computer
Control Panel
Devices and Printers
Default Program
Help and Suppo

Shut down ▸

Switch user
Log off
Lock
Restart
Sleep
Hibernate

Instead, you can click ▸ *(also circled). A box appears as shown offering other choices:*

- *If there are multiple user accounts on the computer, you can click* **Switch user** *to log in to a different one. Your current session stays open and you can switch back to it later on.*

- *You can click* **Log off** *to end your session and log in as a different user without turning the computer off.*

  If the other user has a password, you'll need to know it to switch to or log into their account.

- *You can click* **Lock** *to hide your current session. You'll need to type in your user password to get back to it.*

- *Clicking* **Restart** *shuts the computer down, then reboots it immediately. You can use this if the computer is behaving strangely and you think restarting it might help.*

- *Clicking **Sleep** shuts down the CPU and most other parts of the computer, keeping programs and open documents in the RAM. When you start the computer again, it's ready to use in a few seconds but, until then, it continues drawing a small amount of power (e.g. from its battery if it's a laptop) to keep the RAM working. If power is lost or the battery runs down, you could lose recent changes to the documents. It's wise to save them before putting the computer in Sleep.*

- *You can click **Hibernate**. This is like Sleep but it saves data in the RAM to a special part of the hard disk so the computer can fully power down. Starting up again takes longer than with Sleep but it's still quicker than if you turn the computer off completely.*

What you learned:

- **How to turn off the computer correctly and why you should always do this.**

- *How to Sleep or Hibernate the computer and what these do.*

- *Two ways to switch to a different user's account.*

4 Basics of word processing

This chapter shows how to type text into a new document, make changes to it, do some basic formatting, save the document on the hard disk and print it. You'll also learn some important concepts, terms and techniques.

The document made in this chapter will be used again in Chapter 10.

4.1 Starting Word

Click the 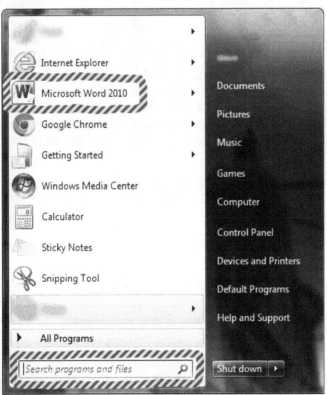 orb, then click in the *Search programs and files* box (circled below) and type *word*. Click *Microsoft Word 2010* in the list that appears above the box.

Once you've used Word a few times, Windows may add it to the list of programs above All Programs that appears when you click 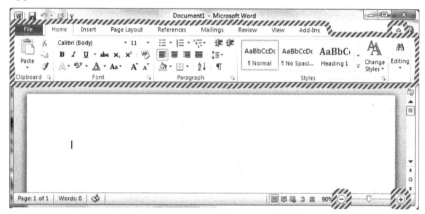*. Once it's in that list (as shown above), you can start it quickly by clicking on it there.*

You've copied the Word program from the hard disk into RAM. There may be a few seconds delay before it starts running and a window appears on the screen.

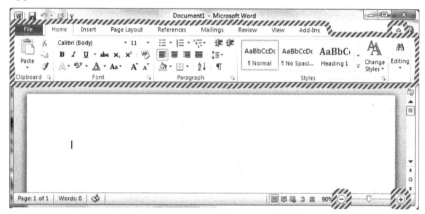

At the top of the window is the **titlebar** showing the name of the program and the document that's open. There are the usual three buttons at the right-hand end of the titlebar and there are some small icons at the left hand end. You can drag the window (unless it's maximised) by putting the mouse cursor anywhere over the titlebar away from the icons and buttons.

Below the titlebar is the **ribbon** (circled) containing various icons arranged in groups. Each group has a different tab above the ribbon: the *Home* one is shown here.

You can see another group of icons by clicking on a different tab.

The ribbon is new in Office 2010. Older versions of Microsoft Office, along with LibreOffice, use drop-down menus instead. If you have one of these, you should use the version of this book that covers Office 2003 or LibreOffice.

The ribbon occupies a lot of screen space and takes some learning if you're used to drop-down menus but it makes many things easier. You can minimise it so only the tabs show by clicking ⌃ *(circled) – it reappears when you click on a tab.*

There's all or part of a white page on a grey background in the Word window below the ribbon. The page may be too large or too small to see comfortably. If so, click repeatedly on one of the circled **zoom** buttons to make it bigger or smaller. ⊕ makes it bigger, ⊖ makes it smaller.

What you learned:

- **How to start Word.**
- **What a titlebar is.**
- **How to change the size of the page on the screen by zooming.**
- **What the ribbon is.**
- *How to minimise it.*
- *That this is the wrong version of this book if you aren't using a version of Office that has the ribbon.*

4.2 Typing, copying and pasting text

Click anywhere on the blank page. There should be a flashing vertical line near the top left. This is the **text cursor** which shows where anything you type will go.

Type *The quick brown fox jumps over the lazy dog. X*. We'll be referring to a sequence of letters like this as **text**.

> *The text is stored as a series of bytes in your computer's RAM. If you pulled out the computer's power plug now (don't try it), it would be lost.*

Move the mouse cursor to just before the X that you just typed. Hold down the left mouse button and drag the cursor leftwards to the start of the word *The*. The text you dragged the cursor over is highlighted: it's shown with a blue background. The **highlighting** shows that it's **selected**.

Move the mouse cursor over  (one of the circled icons on the ribbon) and click.

> *This copies the highlighted text to the **clipboard**. Imagine making a copy of a paper tape containing the highlighted words.*

> *If you can't see the icons shown above, try maximising the window and clicking on the Home tab (circled).*

Move the mouse cursor over (another of the circled icons). After a short delay, a small box (shown above) appears describing what the icon does. This is a **tooltip**.

> *Icons in various programs have tooltips.*

Notice *(Ctrl+V)* in the tooltip. This is a **keyboard shortcut**. Pressing these keys together does the same as moving the mouse cursor and clicking on the icon.

You can use that keyboard shortcut now. Hold down the CTRL key and press *V* five times.

> *The first time you press CTRL+V, it removes the highlighted text, **pastes** a copy of the text on the clipboard in its place and places the text cursor at the end of it. In this case, the text was replaced with a copy of itself but the highlighting was removed. You could do the same thing by moving the mouse cursor to the end of the highlighted text and clicking.*

> *The next four times you press CTRL+V, another copy is inserted at the cursor position.*

The keyboard shortcut to copy text to the clipboard (also shown in the tooltip for 🖹) is Ctrl+C.

Release the CTRL key. The text cursor should be after the pasted sentences and just in front of the *X*. Press DELETE. *X* disappears.

Word has a feature called Intellisense which tries to anticipate what you want to do and make it easier. Unfortunately it often does exactly the opposite. In this case, if you try to select the sentence and space without having something unselected after it (i.e. the X), Intellisense insists on putting each pasted sentence in a separate paragraph.

You might not be able to see the text cursor or the X after pasting if Word puts a little box (🖹 (Ctrl) ▼) over it. Press the ESC key to get rid of the box.

Press RETURN. The text cursor moves down. Type *What do these dogs like?*.

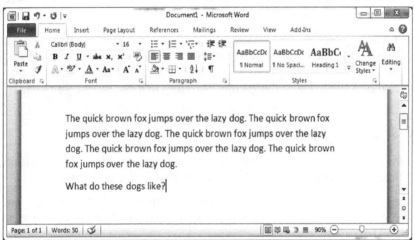

Why is this document such drivel? It's so you don't have to spend much time typing it in and you won't be distracted thinking about what it says and how you could improve it.

What you learned:

- **How to start typing a document.**
- **How to select (highlight) text by dragging with the mouse.**
- **How to copy selected text to the clipboard.**
- **What tooltips are.**

- **What keyboard shortcuts are.**
- **What *Press CTRL+V* means.**
- **How to paste text from the clipboard.**
- *That any existing highlighted text is replaced with pasted text.*
- *What Intellisense is and that it can be annoying.*

4.3 Using the Ribbon

You'll notice that, for each tab on the ribbon, the icons and drop-down boxes are organised into groups with a name underneath. For example, the *Home* tab has *Clipboard*, *Font*, *Paragraph*, *Styles* and *Editing* groups.

In future, where you need to click on an icon on the ribbon, we'll show the icon and which tab and group it is in. If the icon is a bit hard to identify, its tooltip is added. E.g. to copy something to the clipboard, click ⬛ (*Home/Clipboard - Copy*).

Sometimes there isn't enough space on the ribbon to show all the icons. In that case, only the names for some groups appear, along with a downwards pointing triangle (▾). Clicking on the triangle shows a box containing the icons in the group. You can click on the one you need.

4.4 Making changes

You saw that a flashing cursor (a vertical line) appears at the position where anything you type will be placed. This is the **text cursor**.

You can place it by moving the mouse cursor to the position you want and clicking. Try this to place the flashing cursor after the word *jumps* in the first sentence.

You can also use the four arrow keys (Section 3.2) to move the flashing text cursor. Press the one pointing to the right several times to move the cursor past the word *over*.

Press DELETE three times. Each time you press the key, Word removes one letter from your document and moves all the ones after it back one place. You could imagine snipping a row of holes out of a paper tape and gluing it back together but the computer does this so quickly it seems instantaneous.

You should have got rid of the word *the* but you might have got rid of a space and the *t* and *h* instead so that you see the word *overe*. It depends whether you started with the cursor before or after the space. If the *e* is still there, press DELETE again to get rid of it, then press SPACEBAR to restore the space that you accidentally deleted.

Type *some*. Word inserts the word *some* into the document at the position of the cursor.

> *You can add text to your document any time you want to. Just put the cursor where you want it to go and start typing.*

You changed a word in the first sentence but it's still wrong. Press BACKSPACE four times. Just like DELETE, it deletes a letter each time you press it but it's the letter before the text cursor instead of the one after it.

Type *a*. Now the sentence is what you want: *The quick brown fox jumps over a lazy dog.*

What you learned:

- **How to reposition the text (flashing) cursor with the mouse.**
- **How to move the text cursor using the arrow keys.**
- **The computer inserts and deletes letters at the position of the text cursor.**
- **BACKSPACE deletes the letter before the flashing cursor.**
- **DELETE deletes the letter after the flashing cursor.**

4.5 Finding and replacing

You changed the first sentence to read *a lazy dog*. You could change the next four sentences the same way but computers are supposed to make things easier.

Move the mouse cursor (not the flashing text cursor) over the offending *the* in the second sentence and double-click. The word becomes highlighted (its background colour changes). Double-clicking automatically selects a whole word.

Click ᵃᵇᵃᵈ Replace (*Home/Editing* on the ribbon). The *Find and Replace* dialogue box appears as shown a bit later on.

> *A **dialogue box** is a small to medium sized window that appears when you're doing certain things. It shows information and may*

allow you to make various choices before clicking on a button to continue what you're doing

Remember that 🔧 Replace might not be visible on the ribbon and you may need to click 🔭 Editing to see it.

Some icons shown in this book are rearranged to fit better. On your screen, you'll see Editing under the binoculars.

In *Find what:* in the dialogue box, the word *the* is shown – that's the text that it's ready to look for. If you wanted, you could edit the text.

Click [More >>]. Additional options appear. Click on the tickbox next to *Match case* (circled below) so that a tick appears as shown below, then click in the *Replace with:* box (also circled) and type *a*.

*A dialogue box can have multiple **tickboxes** enabling various options. You can tick any combination of these depending on what you want to happen. Clicking again in a box that's ticked clears it.*

Word is now ready to search through our document, replacing *the* with *a* when it finds it. Because you ticked *Match case,* it won't change *The* at the start of each sentence. Put the mouse cursor over the *Find & Replace* dialogue box's titlebar and drag the box so that you can see the text in the document.

Click [Replace]. This moves to and highlights the next *the.*

Illogically, Word doesn't replace the text that was initially highlighted.

Click [Replace] again. This changes *the* to *a* and highlights the next *the.* Suppose you don't want to change that one. Click [Find Next]. Word leaves it unchanged and highlights the one after.

*Click 🔭 Find ▾ (Home/Editing) if you just want to find a particular word, phrase or name in your document. All matching text is highlighted in the document. A Navigation **task pane** opens showing text surrounding each match. You can quickly spot the one you want and click it to go there in the document itself.*

When you've finished with the task pane, click ✖ in its top right corner to close it.

Let's be brave and click [Replace All]. That changes any remaining words *the* to *a*. When asked whether to continue searching at the beginning, click [Yes].

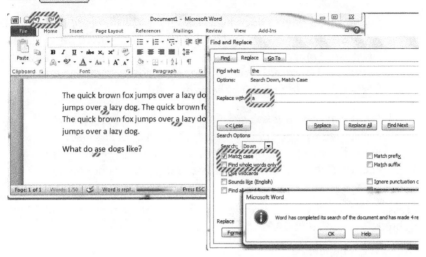

Uh-oh. Word changed *the* in places you wanted to leave unchanged and it also changed *the* in the word *these* so it now reads *ase*. You could have avoided the last unwanted change by also ticking *Find whole words only* but it's too late now.

Click on [OK], then on [Close] to close the *Find and Replace* box.

Click ↰ (Undo - circled above at the top left). If you prefer, just press the shortcut key which is CTRL+Z.

Word remembers each change that you make to your document. **Undo** undoes them one by one. You've undone the changes you made when you clicked [Replace All]. Don't bother trying to redo them.

> *There's a limit to how many changes you can undo but it's generous. If you accidentally undo more changes than you intended, you can **redo** them by clicking ↻ (also circled). Unfortunately you can only redo changes in the same order you made them originally: there isn't a way to skip some of them.*
>
> *[Replace All] is always a dangerous button to click. If you haven't carefully thought out all the possible places that something might match the Find what: text, unexpected things can get changed too. In a long document, you might not spot this until it was too late to undo the changes. All the same, [Replace All] saves time if you need to make a lot of changes in the document and*

the Find what: text is unusual (e.g. a misspelled word where you've taken care to tick Find whole words only).

Suppose you have a document describing the duties of two people: Alice and Bob. You decide their roles should be swapped. You can't just start by using Replace All *to change Alice to Bob everywhere. If you do that, Bob will have all the jobs and* Replace All *could only give them all to Alice.*

What you can do is to use Replace All *to change Alice to a nonsense sequence of characters that never occur elsewhere in your document, e.g. abcxyz. You can then use* Replace All *to change Bob to Alice and finally use it again to change abcxyz to Bob.*

Press CTRL+A. All the text in the document is selected and high-lighted. Press SPACEBAR.

Oops. What happened?

The text you just selected (the whole document in this case) was replaced with a single space. Don't panic. 🥄 or CTRL+Z undoes that mistake too.

What you learned:

- **How to quickly select (highlight) a word.**
- **What a dialogue box is and how to move it.**
- **What tickboxes are and how to tick and clear them.**
- **That Word can search for a particular sequence of letters, e.g. a word, part of a word or a phrase (several words with spaces in between).**
- **That Word can quickly and easily replace that sequence with something different.**
- **That Word can do this everywhere in your document in an instant.**
- **That the computer does exactly what you tell it to do, even if that isn't what you wanted.**
- **You can undo recent changes to your document if something goes wrong.**
- **This includes the heart-stopping case where your document disappears completely because you accidentally replaced it all with a single space.**

- *You can redo changes if you accidentally undo too many of them.*

- *How to quickly find all occurrences of some text.*

- *What a task pane is and how to close it.*

- *How to use* Replace All *to swap two words such as names.*

- *That some icons shown in this book are rearranged to fit better.*

4.6 Selecting

You've seen a number of ways to select words in a document. Selecting is something you'll do often and it's useful to know how to do it quickly and easily.

- You can select text in a document by placing the mouse cursor at one end of it, then holding down the left mouse button and dragging to the other end of the selection.

- You can select everything in a document by pressing CTRL+A or by clicking ⬚ Select ▾ (*Home/Editing*), then clicking ⬚ Select All in the box that appears.

- In Word, double-clicking selects a word while triple-clicking selects a whole paragraph. Other programs may be slightly different but you can always try clicking and see what happens.

After you've selected something, you can **extend** the selection by holding down SHIFT and clicking where you want the selection to start or end. For example, suppose you want to select several pages of a document. You can't see them all on the screen at the same time and selecting by dragging with the mouse is tricky. Instead, select the first word you want on the first page, then use the scroll bar to go to and see the last word you want in the selection. While holding down SHIFT, click just after it.

There are many things you can do with a selection. You can delete it using either the DELETE or BACKSPACE key. You can replace it with whatever is on the clipboard using ⬚ or CTRL+V (Paste). You can also replace selected text by typing something new.

You can put a selection on the clipboard using ✄ or CTRL+X (Cut) or using ⬚ or CTRL+C (Copy). **Cut** moves the selection to the clipboard. **Copy** leaves the selection in place and puts a new copy on the clipboard.

What you learned:

- **Things can be selected by dragging over them or, in many cases, clicking on them.**
- **You can extend a selection by holding down SHIFT and clicking.**
- **You can select everything in the document by pressing CTRL+A or by clicking** ⬚ Select ▾ **and** ⬚ Select All **.**
- **You can delete a selection with DELETE or BACKSPACE.**
- **The difference between cutting and copying something to the clipboard.**

There are many more things you can do with selections that you'll be seeing later on.

4.7 Paragraphs, margins, indents and tabs

Before you typed the last line of the document, you pressed the RETURN key. Pressing RETURN tells Word to start a new paragraph.

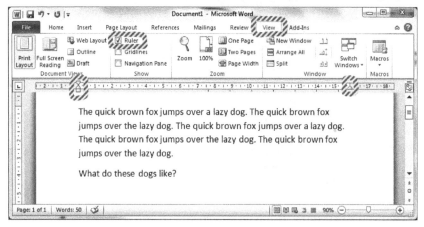

Click the *View* tab (circled) to see the View icons on the ribbon. Click in the box to the left of *Ruler* (also circled) so it's ticked as shown. **Rulers** appear above and to the left of the document.

Remember: in future, we'll just say Tick Ruler (View/Show).

At each end of the ruler above the document, there are small sliders circled above. Click to place the text cursor anywhere in the first paragraph, then try dragging the sliders along the rulers.

The one at the right hand end sets the right margin. As it's dragged to the left, lines of text in the first paragraph get shorter.

The top slider at the left sets the starting position for the first line in the paragraph. Dragging the bottom slider at the left sets the starting position for the remaining lines in the paragraph.

> *There's also a ruler at the left hand side. Numbers on the rulers show distances on the printed page (they may be different on the screen). Screenshots in this book have the rulers set to show distances in centimetres.*

If you drag the bottom left slider away from the left-hand end of the ruler, you can position the top left slider to its left. This **outdents** the first line of the paragraph – something you might occasionally want to do.

The sliders are only affecting the first paragraph because that's where you put the text cursor. If you had selected all or part of a number of paragraphs (or all of them with CTRL+A), the sliders would affect all the selected paragraphs at the same time.

Drag all the sliders back to where they originally were, then drag the top left one to the right to **indent** the paragraph.

Click after the question mark after *like* to put the text cursor there. Press TAB and type *Walkies*. Press TAB again and type *Chasing things*. Press RETURN, then TAB, and type *Eating*. Press TAB again and type *Barking*. Press TAB again and type *Sleeping*.

> **Tab** *is an abbreviation of Tabulator. This is a key on a traditional typewriter that's used when typing a table.*

Drag the mouse to select part or all of the last two lines. Click on the ruler above the start of the word *Walkies*. ▙ appears on the ruler and *Walkies* and *Eating* both start below it. Click on the ruler again a bit to the right of *Walkies*. Another ▙ appears and *Chasing things* and *Barking* both start below it. You've set two tab stops.

> *There are default tab stops to the right of the two that you set. Sleeping is lined up with one of them.*

> *You can use tabs to arrange text in columns.*

Drag the ▙ marks along the ruler and the text below in both lines moves with them. The lines are separate paragraphs because you pressed RETURN between them but, as when setting indents, tab changes affect all selected paragraphs.

To get rid of a tab stop, place the mouse pointer over its ◣ , hold down the left mouse button and drag it down away from the ruler.

When you outdent a paragraph, the bottom left slider also acts as a tab stop. For example, if you're typing a glossary, you can set up outdenting and press TAB after each word that you define. The first word of its definition will line up with the start of subsequent lines.

If you double-click any of the tab stops on the ruler, a dialogue box opens where you see a list of all the tab stops you've set. You can choose one of them by its position and change its type. With the usual Left stop, the first character following the tab will be aligned with the stop. The other stop types work on all the text you type following the tab up to another tab or the end of the line. A Right stop aligns the end of the text with the stop and a Center stop centres it on the stop. A Decimal stop is similar to a Right stop but, if the text contains a decimal point, it's aligned with the stop. This is used to set up a column of numbers, e.g. prices.

A Bar stop doesn't affect the alignment of the text but it causes a vertical line to appear at its position which you can use to separate columns of text.

What you learned:

- **Pressing RETURN starts a new paragraph.**
- **How to see a different group of icons on the ribbon.**
- **How to make the rulers appear.**
- **How to set the left and right margins.**
- **How to indent or outdent paragraphs.**
- **How to set and adjust tabs to create columns of text.**
- **That, if you don't set tab stops, default tab positions are used.**
- **That margins, indents and outdents and tabs can apply to one, several or all paragraphs in a document.**
- *How to change the dimension units on the ruler.*

- *How to remove a tab stop.*
- *An easy way to format a glossary.*
- *The difference between a Left, Right, Centred and Decimal tab stop.*

4.8 Word Wrapping and Justification

You'll have noticed, when you adjusted the right margin of the first paragraph of the document, that Word automatically chose the word beginning each line of the paragraph so that the previous line fitted nicely. This is automatic **word-wrapping**.

The lines in a paragraph are also automatically adjusted when you add or delete text or if you change the text font, which you'll be doing soon.

You can see why you should only press RETURN when you want to start a new paragraph. Not only don't you need to press RETURN at the end of a line within a paragraph, doing it causes problems. Word treats the next line as a new paragraph and the word-wrapping won't work correctly if you make changes later.

> *There are times when you want to start a new line without it starting a new paragraph. Holding down SHIFT and pressing RETURN does this: it's called a **line break**.*

> *Holding down CTRL and pressing RETURN starts a new paragraph on a new page. This is known as a **page break**.*

When Word decides to start a new line in a paragraph, it's unlikely that the previous line will be exactly the right length to extend to the right-hand margin. Usually, it'll be a bit shorter. There are four ways to deal with the leftover space.

The simplest answer is to leave it all at the right hand end of the line. All lines start at the left hand margin but most end a bit before the right-hand one. This is known as **left-justified**: it's what you've used so far.

Things can be reversed so that the leftover space is on the left hand side and all lines end at the right margin. This is **right-justified** text – it isn't used often.

Another option is to split the leftover space equally between the two ends of each line so that the line is **centred** between the margins.

The last option is to add the leftover space equally between words on the line and sometimes also between letters in each word. This allows each line to start at the left margin and end exactly at the right margin too. It's known as **fully-justified** text. Newspapers, magazines and books often use full justification but it can look too formal in other documents.

You've probably spotted that each of these four paragraphs uses the justification that it describes: left, right, centred and full.

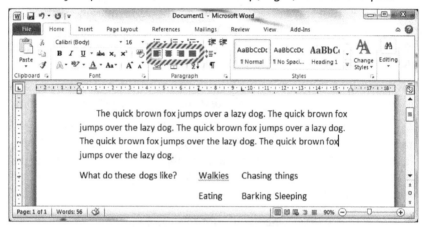

To set the justification for one or more paragraphs, place the cursor there or select the paragraphs, then click one of the four icons circled in the picture above (*Home/Paragraph*).

What you learned:

- **How word-wrapping works.**
- **Why you should only press RETURN to start a new paragraph.**
- **What text justification is and how to set it. This includes centring text.**
- *How to start a new line within a paragraph by pressing SHIFT+RETURN.*
- *How to start a new page by pressing CTRL+RETURN.*

4.9 Styles, Typefaces and Fonts

In the screenshot later in this section, two drop-down **selector boxes** are circled along with three **style** icons below them (*Home/Font*).

Drag over the first and second sentences of the first paragraph to select them, then click **B** (one of the circled icons) or press the equivalent keyboard shortcut: CTRL+B. The words become darker and more prominent – **the style is now Bold**.

Click the mouse anywhere in the document to unselect the two sentences, then select the first sentence on its own. **B** is still highlighted, showing that the words are in bold. Click the icon. It's no longer highlighted and the first sentence is back to normal. The second sentence is still in bold.

> *Each time you click one of the three style icons, the style is either applied to or removed from the selected text.*

Select the third sentence and click *I* (another circled icon) or press CTRL+I. The words are slanting – *the style is Italic*.

Select the fourth sentence and click **U** (the third circled icon) or press CTRL+U. <u>The sentence is underlined</u>.

> *If you click ▼ to the right of **U**, you can choose different underlining styles.*

Select the fifth sentence and click all three icons in succession. <u>***The sentence is in bold and italic and it is also underlined***</u>.

> *You can use any combination of the three icons or any combination of the keyboard shortcuts one after another.*

Drag the mouse or triple-click to select the whole of the first paragraph. Press CTRL+C to copy it, including its end-of-paragraph marker, to the clipboard. Press CTRL+V three times so that there are three copies of the paragraph.

Select the whole of the second copy by dragging the mouse or by triple-clicking in it, then go to the box circled below showing the number *16* (on your screen, it'll probably show 11). Click ▼ to its right and then on the number *20* in the drop-down list that appears. All the words in the second paragraph get bigger. We changed the paragraph to 20 point.

> *The size of printed characters is traditionally given in **points**, measured from the top of a tall character such as h to the bottom of a descender, e.g. in j. A point is 1/72 of an inch (0.353 mm). 10 point is the smallest size you should normally use – anything smaller could be classed as "fine print" although newspapers often use smaller print and are still quite legible. 12*

point is easier to read and you'll want to use larger sizes again for headings, etc.

Word normally defaults to 10, 11 or 12 point text. Screenshots prepared for this book use 16 point text to make it easier to see.

Select the third paragraph, then go to the box circled below showing *Calibri (Body)*. Click ▼ to its right. A list of **typefaces** installed on your computer appears. There may be too many to show them all. If so, there will be a scrollbar next to the list. Scroll down, find *Cambria* and click on it.

The typeface of the third paragraph changes from **Calibri** to **Cambria**.

Cambria is a serif typeface: the letters have small lines across their ends.

Calibri is a simpler **sans-serif** typeface.

*Calibri and Cambria are **proportional** fonts – each letter is just as wide as it needs to be. The widest letter is m, others such as i are narrower.*

*Another typeface worth mentioning is **Courier**. This is a **mono-spaced** font – all letters are spaced far enough apart for an m to fit.*

`Courier looks as if it was typed on a typewriter.`

*In traditional printing, a **font** is a box of cast metal letters of a particular typeface, point size and style (e.g. italic) but people often say font when they mean typeface. For example, they might say to use Times New Roman as the font for a document that contains text of various styles and point sizes.*

Windows uses its installed fonts to convert the letter codes stored by programs running on the computer into the shape of the corresponding letter on the screen or on paper in the printer. For example, the letter A is stored in memory as a single byte (8 bits) but this code is converted to a pattern of several hundred or thousand dots to make the shape of an A on the screen or on paper with a particular typeface, point size and style.

Sometimes Windows has different versions of a font installed to produce the different styles. If not, it modifies the normal style of the font (e.g. by widening the lines or slanting the characters).

Depending which fonts are installed, you may have many typefaces in the list - some of them very fancy.

You'll have problems if a document is moved to a different computer that doesn't have a font that you used installed on it. This often happens if you e-mail the document to someone else. Their computer will automatically choose a similar font that it does have installed but the match may not be good.

*Courier and **Times New Roman** are usually present on any Windows computer along with the sans-serif **Arial**. Older computers may not have Cambria and Calibri (default fonts in Windows Vista and 7). You may want to use Arial and Times New Roman instead of Calibri and Cambria to avoid problems.*

You can highlight individual words or even letters within a word and change their typeface, size and style.

As a rule of thumb, you should avoid using more than two or three different typefaces in the same document. Using too many looks messy.

Drag to select the first sentence of the third paragraph. Click **Aa**˅ (*Home/Font* - circled below). Click on UPPERCASE in the small box that appears. The sentence changes to all capitals.

Other choices are Sentence case where only the first letter of a sentence is capitalised, all lowercase and Capitalize Each Word. tOGGLE cASE is useful if you typed something without noticing that CAPS LOCK was on.

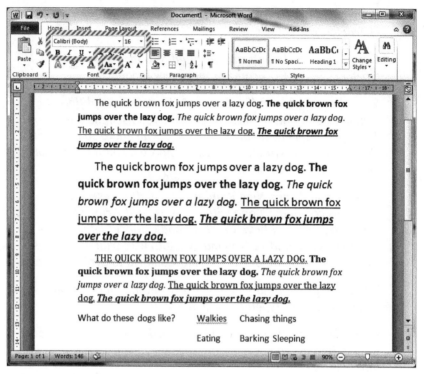

What you learned:

- **What text styles are and how to set and unset them.**
- **That text styles can be used in any combination.**
- **What a typeface is.**
- **How to change the size and typeface of text.**
- **The difference between serif and sans-serif typefaces.**
- **How to change the capitalisation of text.**
- *The difference between proportional and mono-spaced typefaces.*
- *That text size is measured in points.*
- *What a font is (it can mean two different things) and how the computer uses it.*
- *That you can have problems with fonts when a document is opened on a different computer.*

Chapter 4 Basics of word processing

- *That you might want to use Arial and Times New Roman typefaces so your documents display correctly on older computers.*
- *Not to go overboard with too many different typefaces.*

4.10 Symbols

To insert a special symbol that isn't on your keyboard, click Ω Symbol ▾ (*Insert/Symbols* on the ribbon).

A box appears containing some commonly used symbols such as ©. Clicking one of these inserts it at the text cursor position.

You can select from a much wider choice of symbols by clicking Ω More Symbols... in the box. A dialogue box appears where you can choose a font.

Ordinary fonts such as Calibri and Cambria include commonly used symbols and foreign alphabets (e.g. Greek). Special fonts such as Webdings and Wingdings contain symbols like 👪 or 🌐 instead of letters.

Once you've chosen a font, you see the available characters and symbols. You'll need to scroll up or down to see them all. Click on the one you want, then click [Insert] to insert it at the text cursor position.

The dialogue box stays open. You can drag it so you can see your document, click somewhere else in it and insert another symbol there. Once you've finished, click [Close] to close the dialogue box.

> You can copy and paste a symbol already in your document anywhere else that you need it. Double-clicking on a symbol from a special font opens the Symbol dialogue box: you can see which font it's in. If you need a related symbol it'll probably be available in that font too.

> Symbols are stored in memory just like letters: it's the font selection that makes them look different. If you accidentally change the typeface for some of your text to a symbol font such as Wingdings, it'll start showing as meaningless symbols. Don't panic, just change it back.

What you learned:

- **How to find and insert the symbols you want into your document.**

- **That ordinary fonts can include foreign alphabets and some symbols.**

- **That Windows has special fonts which contain symbols instead of letters.**

- *How to find related symbols that may be available in the same font.*

- *That you can copy and paste symbols.*

- *What happens if you accidentally select a symbol font.*

4.11 Non-printing characters

You'll remember that the teleprinter machine in Chapter 2 punched a special pattern of holes in the tape when the spacebar was pressed and that this moved the print position on by one place without printing anything when the words on the tape were printed. Other special patterns would be punched if the TAB or RETURN keys were pressed. Your computer stores these same patterns as special characters (bytes) in its memory when you press those keys.

> *Two different special characters can be stored when the RETURN key is pressed. Carriage Return (CR) tells a teleprinter to move its printing position to the start of the line and Line Feed (LF) tells it to advance the paper to a new line. Windows stores the CR-LF sequence when RETURN is pressed while Unix-based systems including Linux and Apple's OS-X store LF only. Older Apple systems store CR only. This can cause problems when files produced by some programs are transferred between different types of computer. Fortunately, files created by Word don't suffer from this problem.*

Click ¶ (*Home/Paragraph*, circled below). You'll see apparent changes in your document. There's a small dot between most of the words. You'll see → between words where you pressed TAB and you'll see a paragraph marker (¶) wherever you pressed RETURN.

> *A common minor mistake is to unintentionally put more than one space between words when typing. With non-printing characters visible, you can spot extra dots where they shouldn't be and delete them.*

You can also use *Replace to get rid of unwanted spaces, whether they're visible or not. Put the cursor in the Find what: box and press the spacebar twice. Put the cursor in the Replace with: box and press the spacebar once. You can now track down any unintentional sequences of two (or more) spaces and get rid of one of them by clicking* Replace *.*

Select the word *Barking* by double-clicking it. Place the mouse cursor over it and press and hold down the left mouse or trackpad button. While still holding the button down, move the cursor between → and *Eating*. Release the button.

You see *Barking Eating*. You moved the highlighted word by dragging and dropping but it's not right. Press CTRL+Z to undo it.

Intellisense added the space between Barking and Eating.

Place the mouse cursor just before *Barking* and drag to just before *Sleeping*. *Barking* is now highlighted along with the → after it: the word is selected along with the special TAB character. Retry dragging and dropping it to just before *Eating*. This time, it works properly: *Barking* and *Eating* are lined up with the tab marks on the ruler.

You can also copy selected text by dragging and dropping. Hold down the CTRL key while dragging. The original selected text remains and a copy is dropped at the cursor position.

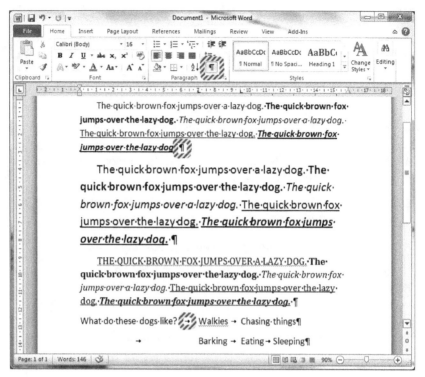

Instead of clicking ¶ on the ribbon, you can turn the special markers on and off by pressing CTRL+*. Try pressing this several times (you'll usually need to hold down SHIFT too). The markers appear and disappear. Leave them off.

The markers for non printing characters won't appear when you print your document, even when they're visible on the screen.

Dragging and dropping and other editing such as replacing highlighted text or cutting and copying it to the clipboard works just the same when the special markers are not visible. If you want to include a space, tab or paragraph marker, you need to highlight the blank space on the screen where the marker would be.

Other non-printing characters are used to record changes in the text formatting such as different indents, justification, typefaces and text styles and sizes. Although they can't be made visible, they're also moved by cutting or copying and pasting or by dragging and dropping. The results of this aren't always what you'd expect or want. In particular, you should keep an eye on the text that was before and after something that you move to make sure that it doesn't change in an unexpected way.

What you learned:

- **What non-printing characters are.**
- **How to make non printing characters visible on the screen.**
- **How to move or copy selected (highlighted) text by dragging and dropping.**
- **That you may need to include non printing characters when you move text around.**
- *That text formatting also uses non printing characters that you can't make visible.*
- *That these can cause problems when you move text.*
- *That different computers use incompatible ways of recording when RETURN is pressed.*
- *How to find and remove unintentional extra spaces between words.*

4.12 Checking your spelling

Try deliberately misspelling a word in the document, then move the text cursor elsewhere. Word looks to see if the word is in its dictionary. When it can't find it, it puts a wavy red line under it. Move the mouse cursor over the offending word and right-click.

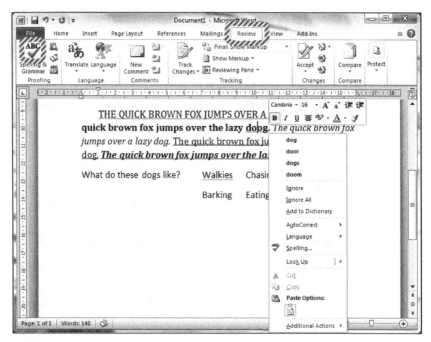

You see a list of possible replacements for the word. Click on the correct one. The word is replaced.

You'll notice that *Walkies* has a wavy red line. This is because it isn't in the dictionary but it doesn't mean that you must change the word. The wavy line won't appear when you print the document. If you want to, right-click the word and choose *Ignore All* to ignore all instances of the word in the document. You can use *Add to Dictionary* to add the word to the dictionary so that it will be accepted in all your documents.

> *You can have multiple spell-check dictionaries installed, e.g. for different languages.*

> *Spell checkers can't spot cases where you've used a wrong sound-alike word that's also in the dictionary. E.g. "I ran this threw the spell chequer sew I know its write".*

You'll also notice that the sentence you changed to UPPERCASE has a wavy green line under it. Word has a grammar checker and it thinks something might be wrong with the sentence. It can spot many other errors such as a sentence without a verb.

If you click ABC (*Proofing* on the *Review* tab, circled above), Word checks the whole document for misspelled words and possible grammatical errors. When it finds one, it shows a dialogue box where you can make the same choices as above. This saves you from having to go through the whole document looking for wavy lines.

What you learned:

- **What the wavy red and green lines mean and what to do about them.**
- **How to spell and grammar check the whole document.**
- *What a spell-checker can't do.*

4.13 Saving the document

Click ⊟ at the top left (circled below) or press the CTRL+S shortcut. The *Save As* dialogue box opens.

> *Even though floppy disks are rarely used any more, the ⊟ icon lives on.*

> *Alternatively click the ribbon's File tab. Unlike the other ribbon tabs which allow you to work on the contents of the document, File fills the whole window with various information, commands and options relating to the document as a whole. Microsoft calls this the **Backstage view**. Click ⊟ Save (circled below).*

You haven't given the document a name yet so Word has chosen one based on the start of the document. It's highlighted but it's not very convenient. You can just type a suitable name, e.g. *LazyDog*. Click [Save] or just press RETURN.

> *When an on-screen button is highlighted, you can press RETURN instead of clicking it.*

> *The document is copied from your computer's RAM to its hard disk. Now it's safely stored as a file even if the computer crashes, is turned off or decides to restart after an update.*

> *Word saves documents in your Documents library but you can choose a different location if you want.*

> *Word normally automatically saves any changes you've made to a special file every 10 minutes or so. If it or the computer crashes or there's a power failure, you'll be offered the chance to recover your document when you start Word again. Some of your most recent changes may still be lost.*

Now that the document has a name, it shows this instead of *Docu-ment1* on its titlebar. If you make more changes and save it again (e.g. by clicking 🖫), the changed version immediately replaces the one on the hard disk without you being asked for its name. If you want to keep the old version and save the new version in a different folder and/or with a different name, you can click the ribbon's *File* tab and click 🖳 Save As to open the dialogue box.

What you learned:

- **How to give your document a name and save it to the hard disk.**

- **How to save the document again after you've made changes to it.**

- **How to save a new version of the document with a different name.**

- *That clicking the ribbon's File tab fills the entire window with options and information.*

- *That you can recover most of your document after a crash.*

4.14 Printing the document

Things can sometimes go wrong when you try to print a document. You already saved it – it won't be lost even if the computer locks up or crashes.

Click the ribbon's *File* tab, then click *Print* (circled below). The print options appear.

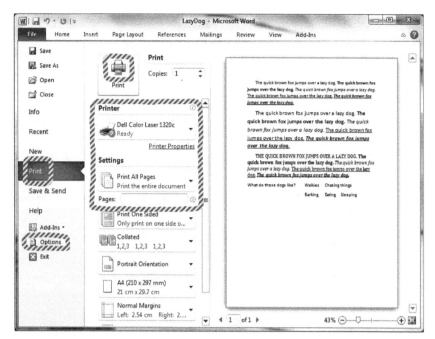

You might have more than one printer set up on your computer. Make sure that the right one is shown: if it isn't, click on ▼, then on the name of the printer you want to use in the list that appears. Make sure that the printer is switched on and isn't out of paper.

If you don't see the printer you want, it may not be installed (set up) on your computer. You'll need to look at the instructions that came with the printer to see how to do this.

You want to print the whole of your document. Check *Print All Pages* is showing, then click 🖨 (circled). The document is printed – perhaps after a short delay.

If you have a long document and don't want to print all of it, type the page numbers you want to print in the box underneath Print All Pages.

The page numbers should be typed with commas between them. You can also specify ranges of pages by putting dashes between them. E.g. 1,3,5-7,10- will print pages 1, 3, 5, 6, 7 and page 10 onwards.

What you learned:

- **How to print a document.**

- **How to select the printer you want to use and the pages you want to print.**

- *That it's wise to save your document before you try to print it.*

4.15 Changing Word options

Click the ribbon's *File* tab, then click ▤ Options (circled in the screen-shot above). A dialogue box opens.

The options are organised in groups which are listed on the left hand side. You may have to look in several groups to find the one you want to change.

For example, to change the rulers to show different units (e.g. inches instead of centimetres, click *Advanced*. Scroll down to find the *Display* group of options. Click ▾ next to *Show measurements in units of:* and click to select *Inches*. Click OK .

> *Many options have ⓘ next to them. Moving the mouse cursor over this shows a short description of what the option does.*

Click X to close Word.

> *If you forget to save the file or if you've made changes since it was last saved, you'll be asked whether you want to save or discard your changes.*

4.16 Documents attached to an e-mail

You can send a file to someone else by **attaching** it to an e-mail. This book doesn't attempt to describe how to send and receive e-mails. There are too many different e-mail programs and systems.

However, there's an important thing you need to know.

Windows has special temporary folders on the hard disk where it keeps files that are only needed for a short time. When you click on a docu-ment on a web page or attached to an e-mail, a copy is put in one of these folders and your word processor is started and told to open it.

Word 2010 on Windows 7 knows that the document is in a temporary folder and opens it in Read Only mode. You'll see this on the titlebar and the *Save As* dialogue box opens when you try to save any changes you've made.

Some other word processors prevent you from making any changes at all until you've saved the document in a safe permanent location. If you're swearing at your computer because it won't let you edit a document, this could be the reason.

However, older versions of Word or **Word 2010 on Windows XP** let you work all day on the document, then click 💾. What you don't realise is that the version with all your changes was written back to the temporary folder. Windows may decide at any time that it's not needed any more and delete it. Even if the file isn't deleted, it's often impossible to find out where it's hidden.

Many people I know have lost hours of work because of this.

Always click 💾 Save As and save the file in a folder such as *Documents* before you start work on any document that you opened directly from an e-mail or web page.

5 Files and folders

This chapter explains how documents, etc. are stored on your computer's hard disk and how to access, organise and move them.

5.1 The hard disk

Click the ⬤ orb, then move the mouse pointer over *Computer* at the right of the box that appears. Click. A window appears.

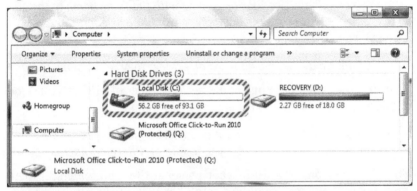

Click on the circled hard disk drive labelled *(C:)* - it may have another name too but this varies. If clicking highlights the drive but doesn't open it, try double clicking it. You should now see a number of icons looking like the folders you'd find in a filing cabinet.

> *You need to be able to select disk drives, folders and files or open them. Windows can be set to use either of two methods:*
>
> * *With the first method, clicking selects a disk drive, folder or file and double-clicking opens it.*
>
> * *With the second method, pausing the mouse cursor over the disk drive, folder or file selects it. This is called* **hover select**. *A single click opens it.*
>
> *Now you know how to open a disk drive, folder or file by clicking on it, we will merely say Open.*

What you're looking at is the **root folder** of your hard disk. There's a *Windows* folder which holds the Windows operating system programs. There's also a *Program Files* folder containing programs you've added.

Don't mess with either of these folders unless you really know what you're doing.

Each folder has a name and it can contain files. A file is like a length of paper tape punched with the bytes that make up the document or program. Imagine that a name is written on it and it's stored in a folder in a filing cabinet.

A folder can contain other folders – this would be useful in a real filing cabinet too but it would be physically hard to achieve.

You can't have two files or folders with the same name in the same folder because the computer would be as confused as you'd be.

*A folder may also be called a **directory**: they're the same thing.*

Open the *Users* folder. You should see a number of folders in it. One of these has your Windows account name. Open it.

Unfortunately, your account and user name may not be the same. You might have to try a couple of different folders.

You now see icons or a list of your personal files and folders. If there are many of them, there will be a scroll bar to the right. Use it to move down until you see folders called *Desktop* and *My Documents*.

Open *My Documents*. You see files and folders. Mentally note some of their names. Your Word document *LazyDog* should be there although you might not spot it immediately.

When you save a new file, Word saves it in My Documents unless you choose a different folder.

Click or double-click on *LazyDog*. It opens: Word starts and displays it. You aren't going to do anything with it. Click ▀ X ▀ to close it and click ▀ X ▀ again to close the *My Documents* folder.

What you learned:

- **What folders and files are.**
- **That they have icons and names.**
- **How to open a folder or a file such as a document.**
- **That you have a personal folder in *Users* with a *Desktop* and a *My Documents* folder in it.**

- **That Word saved the *LazyDog* document in your *My Documents* folder.**

- **That you can start with the root of the hard disk and work your way to any file on the disk but it's tedious**

- *That programs are kept as files in folders that you should leave alone.*

- *That a folder and a directory are the same thing.*

5.2 Finding files and making folders

Click 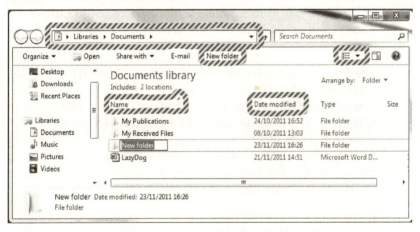, then move the mouse pointer over *Documents* at the right of the box that appears and click. This takes you directly to the folder containing the word processor file – it contains the same files and folders that you just noted. It's a much easier and faster way to get there.

Click ▼ (circled next to ⊟☰). You can choose different ways of showing the files and folders. Click ⊟☰ Details so they appear in a list with *Date Modified* and *Type* as shown above.

If you click on *Name* (circled), the files and folders are sorted alphabetically. The small triangle (▲) above *Name* shows that this is the order. Click on *Name* again. The triangle flips over (▼) and the sorting order is reversed.

Click on *Date Modified* (circled). The triangle appears above this and the files and folders are sorted by the date and time that the last change to them was made. This is very useful if you can't remember the name of a file that you need to find but you know approximately when it was created or changed.

You can sort on any of the other columns instead. Just click on the column title.

Click New folder (circled). A folder appears with the name *New Folder* highlighted. Type *WP files* and press RETURN.

You just made a brand new folder. Its name was set to *New folder* but, because it was highlighted, anything you typed replaced the name and it's now called *WP files*. Open it. Of course it's empty - you only just made it.

Above the list of files is a box (circled) showing the current folder and the folders containing it. You can click on any of those folder names to go to it. Click *Documents* in the box. You're back in the *My Documents* folder.

*Windows 7 usually shows the My Documents, My Music, My Pictures and My Videos folders as **libraries** called Documents, Music, Pictures and Videos. In future, we'll use these library names.*

*The Type column in the list shows whether a file is a program or some kind of data file such as a word processor document or a spreadsheet, picture, sound, etc. Windows knows which type it is because its file name has a dot at the end followed by an **extension**, often three letters. Examples of extensions are .exe for a program, .doc or .docx for a Word document, .jpg for a picture or .mp3 for a music file. Depending on option settings, you may not see the file name extensions.*

*If you open a file whose extension is .exe, Windows knows to copy it into RAM and start running it as a program. Other types of file are **associated** with programs already installed on the computer. When you click on one of those, Windows starts the program and tells it to open the file you clicked on.*

What you learned:

- **My Documents is a special folder – you can get to it quickly via the orb.**
- **You can list the contents of a folder in various orders including by name or by date modified – this helps when you're looking for a file.**
- **A way to create and name a new folder.**

- **The box near the top of the window shows which folders contain the one you're looking at.**

- **You can click on the name of a folder in the box to go to it.**

- *That Windows sometimes refers to some of your folders as "libraries" with slightly different names.*

- *What a file name extension is.*

- *How Windows uses extensions to know the type of a file and what program to use to open it.*

5.3 Using a thumbdrive

If you have a USB thumbdrive / Data Stick, plug it into any USB port on your computer. If in doubt, look at the rectangular metal connector on the thumbdrive, then look for a socket on the front or side of your computer that's the same size and shape.

> *USB (Universal Serial Bus) is a way to connect various devices to the computer including thumbdrives, external hard disks, printers and scanners. Music players, cameras and mobile phones can be connected with USB so you can copy files to and from them.*

After a short delay, a window may appear asking how to use the thumbdrive. You can click ▰ **X** ▰ to close it.

Click ▰, then *Computer*. As before, you see disk *(C:)* but you also see *Removable Disk* lower down. Open it. You'll see folders and files on the thumbdrive (if there are any) – the computer views it as another disk drive.

> *The thumbdrive may have a name which appears instead of Removable Disk.*

Move the mouse cursor over ▰ on the taskbar. A box appears showing *Removable Disk*. It should also show *Documents*. Click on *Documents*. If you don't see it, click ▰ and click *Documents*.

> *To save space on the taskbar, Windows 7 shows a single icon for all the folders you have open. Once you move the mouse cursor over the icon, you see the individual folders in miniature and can click on the one you want.*

Select *LazyDog* by moving the cursor over it or by single-clicking it.

Press CTRL+C to copy *LazyDog* to the clipboard. Move the cursor over [image], click on *Removable Disk* and press CTRL+V. *LazyDog* appears there.

> *Instead of copying and pasting, you could drag LazyDog onto [image], then onto Removable Disk, then release the button to drop it in the Removable Disk window. Windows leaves a copy in Documents because you dragged it from there (on the hard disk) to a different disk.*

Open *LazyDog* on *Removable Disk*. Word starts and displays your document. You aren't going to do anything with it and you can close it.

> *If you wanted, you could make changes to the document but, when they're saved, this will be on the thumbdrive and the copy on the hard disk remains as it was. This quickly gets confusing. There's a risk of ending up with two different copies of the document where some changes are in one and some are in the other.*

Click [image] near the right end of the taskbar, then click *Eject Removable Disk*. Once a message saying *Safe To Remove Hardware* appears, you can unplug the thumbdrive.

> *Saving changes on the thumbdrive can take some time. If you unplug it before "Safe To Remove Hardware" appears, there's a risk of losing files on it.*

> *If you don't see [image], click [image] near the right end of the taskbar. A box containing more icons appears: [image] should be one of them. Click on it.*

If you plug the thumbdrive into a different computer, you can copy files from the thumbdrive to its hard drive. You may not be able to open the files unless the computer has the same programs installed on it. Again of course you must be sure that any changes you make are to the newest version of the document.

Look at the window showing the files in the Documents folder. Notice that *LazyDog* is still there.

What you learned:

- **How to plug in and safely unplug the thumbdrive**
- **That the computer sees it as another disk drive, even though there's no spinning disk.**

- **How to use the clipboard to copy a file such as a word processing document from the hard drive to the thumbdrive.**

- **How to use the thumbdrive to copy a file onto another computer.**

- *How to use the taskbar to switch to a different open folder.*

- *How to drag and drop a file or folder to a different drive.*

- *That, if you do this, Windows makes a new copy and leaves the original file or folder in place.*

- *That you can open and edit a document directly from the thumbdrive but this may not be a good idea.*

5.4 Moving files and creating shortcuts

Position the cursor over *LazyDog* in *Documents*, then hold down the left mouse button. Move the mouse cursor over the new *WP files* folder in the same window, then release the button. *LazyDog* is gone from the *Documents* folder. It was dragged to the *WP files* folder.

Place the cursor over the *WP files* folder and right-click it. In the box that appears, click *Create Shortcut*. *WP files - Shortcut* appears.

Right-click on the new shortcut and, in the box that appears, click on *Cut*. Close the *Documents* window and minimise any other windows that are obscuring the desktop. Right-click on a blank part of the desktop and, in the box that appears, click on *Paste*. *WP files - Shortcut* appears on the desktop.

> *You can cut, copy or paste a file, folder or shortcut using the keyboard shortcut (CTRL+X, CTRL+C or CTRL+V) or by right-clicking.*

> *Files, folders and shortcuts can all be moved by cutting and pasting or by dragging and dropping. You can use whichever method is more convenient.*

> *You can select multiple files and/or folders using CTRL+A, by dragging the mouse cursor over them, by selecting them individually while holding down CTRL or by selecting the first one, then holding down SHIFT and selecting the last one in a list. Once you've selected them, you can copy or move them all at once. Pressing DELETE would delete them.*

Right-click *WP files - Shortcut* and, in the box that appears, click on *Rename*. The name *WP files - Shortcut* is highlighted. Type *WP files* and press RETURN. The name is changed.

Open *WP files* on the desktop by clicking or double-clicking. The *WP files* window reopens, containing *LazyDog*. You can now get there directly from your desktop.

> *A **shortcut file** is a pointer to another file or folder. Its icon includes a little arrow. You can put a shortcut in any folder, not just on the desktop. When you click to open a shortcut, Windows finds the file or folder that it points to and opens that instead.*

Right-click on *LazyDog*, move the cursor over *Send To* and click ■ Desktop (create shortcut) in the box that appears.

> *This is a quicker way to put a shortcut to a file or folder on the desktop. You can rename the new shortcut by right-clicking it on the Desktop and clicking on Rename.*

Click 🔵, then *Computer*. Open *C:*, then *Users*. Open your personal (Windows account) folder as in Section 5.1. Again you see the *Desktop* and *My Documents* folders.

> *You'll also see the My Music, My Pictures and My Videos folders, corresponding to the Music, Pictures and Video libraries (Section 5.2).*

Right-click on *My Documents* and click *Properties*. A dialogue box opens. Click on the *General* tab. The total size of all the files and folders in *My Documents* is shown. This will be useful information when you make a backup copy. Click [Cancel] or ■ X ■ to close the dialogue box.

> *The dialogue box shows both Size and Size on disk. When a file is saved on a disk or thumbdrive, space is allocated in fixed chunks, e.g. 4096 bytes. Usually some of the space in the last chunk ends up unused so the file takes up a bit of additional space on the disk.*

> *You can also see Size (though not Size on disk) by clicking 🔵, right-clicking Documents, then clicking Properties.*

Open the *Desktop* folder. Notice that the two shortcuts you just placed on the desktop are in this folder. *Desktop* is a special folder – anything it in appears on the computer desktop.

As well as shortcuts, you can put documents and folders themselves on the Desktop. Section 5.5 explains why this often isn't a good idea.

Open *LazyDog - Shortcut* by clicking or double-clicking on it on the desktop. Word starts and displays the document. Click ████ **X** ████ to close it.

When a document has a shortcut on the desktop, it's very easy to open it.

You can get rid of a shortcut by right-clicking it and choosing Delete: the file or folder that it points to isn't affected. But be sure it's a shortcut (with the little arrow): the file or folder itself might be on the desktop.

*When you delete a file, folder or shortcut, Windows moves it to the special **Recycle Bin** folder that you'll see on your desktop. If you deleted the file or folder accidentally, you can open the Recycle Bin, find it, right-click it and click Restore.*

You'll want to make folders in Documents and organise your documents in them. It's up to you how to set up the folders: it's like planning a filing cabinet although a bit more flexible. You can get to any of the folders from Documents so you'll only want to put shortcuts on the desktop for the files and folders that you use most often. If you put too many shortcuts there, it gets messy and confusing.

What you learned:

- **How to move a file to a different folder on the same hard disk by dragging and dropping or by cutting and pasting.**
- **How to create a shortcut to a file or folder.**
- **How to get quickly to a folder or open a document by putting a shortcut on the desktop.**
- **That the desktop displays files, folders and shortcuts placed in the special Desktop folder.**
- **How to see the total size of all the files in a folder.**
- *That a file usually takes up a few more bytes than its size when it's saved.*
- *That you can cut, copy or paste a file or folder by right-clicking.*

- *How to select and copy, move or delete multiple files or folders.*
- *How to restore a file or folder that you deleted accidentally.*
- *How to identify and delete a shortcut.*
- *That this doesn't delete the file it points to.*

5.5 Making backups

If the hard disk in your computer fails or if the computer breaks down or is lost or stolen, you could lose all your files. These could include not only documents that you've worked on for weeks but also irreplaceable files such as your photos.

Your personal document files are usually all in *Documents*. You can copy and paste *Documents* to a thumbdrive. Safely remove the thumbdrive and store it away from the computer.

> *You could have dragged WP files to the desktop folder instead of leaving it in Documents and putting a shortcut on the desktop. That's easier to do but its files wouldn't be backed up when you make a copy of Documents.*

> *Don't just drag Documents to the thumbdrive: Windows 7 may only put a useless shortcut there instead of a copy of the folder and files.*

If there's enough space on the thumbdrive, you can update the backup by renaming the old *Documents* folder on it, copying the new version to it, then deleting the old version. If there isn't enough space to do this, you'll have to delete the old version before copying the new version. That's a bit riskier. Make absolutely sure you're deleting the backup *Documents* and not *Documents* on the computer itself!

You might have music, photos and videos in the *Music*, *Pictures* and *Videos* folders. You can copy these folders too. However, they tend to take much more space than your documents and the copies may not fit on the thumbdrive. You can buy an external hard disk instead. It works exactly the same way as the thumbdrive but holds much more data.

You can use two external disks or thumbdrives so that one is always stored safely, even when you're updating files on the other one. Ideally, keep one of them in a different building in case of burglary or fire.

There are two different types of external hard disks available: ones that are powered from the computer and ones that have a separate power supply that needs to be plugged in. The ones with a separate power supply are generally less expensive but also less convenient.

Windows 7 includes a backup program (click 🪟 *and type backup into the Search programs and files box) and there are other programs available that you can use to manage backups. They can save time because they only copy new and changed files to the backup.*

There are services available that back up your files to a server on the Internet. They solve the problem of keeping the backup in a different building. However, if you have confidential information, are you sure no-one is going to snoop in the backup copy?

What you learned:

- **What a backup is and why it's important to make one.**
- **That all that's normally needed is to make a copy of** *Documents* **on a thumbdrive.**
- **That you can use an external hard disk instead of a thumbdrive – it holds more.**
- **That it's a good idea to keep two backups and have one of them in a different building.**
- *Why you should try to keep all your documents in the Documents folder.*
- *That music, pictures and videos are kept in other folders that you may need to back up too.*
- *That there are special programs for making backups which may be faster.*
- *That you can save your backups over the internet.*

5.6 The clipboard

You've used the clipboard to copy text and paste it somewhere else in a document and to cut or copy files and paste them in different folders.

The clipboard is part of Windows and every program can use it, including Word. As well as files, folders and text, it can hold other things such as pictures and spreadsheets as you'll see in Chapter 9. Because it's part of Windows, it can be used to move something from one program to another although only if the program you're pasting it into knows what to do with it.

For example, if you're looking at a web page using a browser program such as Internet Explorer or Firefox, you can select text or even a picture on the page, copy it and paste it into your word processor document. If you have two word processor documents open at once, you can cut or copy text from one document and paste it into the other one.

The clipboard only holds one thing at a time. When you copy something to it, it replaces whatever was there before. There are add-on programs which allow you to keep several things on the clipboard at once but those are outside the scope of this book and they can be confusing.

6 Structuring a document

This chapter covers Word features that make it easier to type a document, format it consistently, give it a structure such as sections or chapters and add headers and footers and a table of contents. It covers additional features such as bullet points and numbered lists and discusses templates.

By now, you should be quite familiar with the ribbon, dialogue boxes, etc. You won't need such detailed instructions and screenshots

6.1 Autocorrection

You need to make a new document containing some extracts from this book. Start Word as in Section 4.1 and type the following into the new document (press RETURN when you see ¶ and don't worry at all about formatting at this stage):

Introduction¶
Are you just starting with a computer to write letters?¶
have

Word spotted that you're starting a new sentence but you didn't capitalise the *H* in *Have*. It's done that for you: this is its **auto-correction** feature. Sometimes it makes changes that you don't want. Just go back and undo the change it made – it'll get the hint. Continue typing:

you been using a word processor for some time but still find it intimidating and feel that you don't understand what it's doing?¶
If you fit either description, this book is meant for you.¶
¶
Behind the screen¶
"I'm buying a new computer. It has:¶
An Intel Dual Core processor¶
4GB (232 bytes) of RAM"¶
Chapters 2-5 of this book are general.¶
¶
Basics of Windows¶
This chapter covers basics such as managing program windows and switching between them.¶
Maybe you already know this.¶
Clicking with the mouse¶

Instead of using the left button, you can click with the right hand one. This has a different effect from normal clicking.¶
It's possible to change settings so the mouse buttons are switched.¶
Starting the Web Browser¶
Click on the orb at the bottom left of the screen.¶
You'll see your choice of web browser program. Click on it.¶

What you learned:

- **What auto correction is and how to override it.**

6.2 Formatting individual characters

The text you typed in shows what 4GB is as a power of two but it needs to be formatted to make sense. Drag to select the second and third digits in *232*. Click **x²** (*Home/Font - Superscript* on the ribbon). The text becomes superscripted: the line reads *4GB (2³² bytes) of RAM"* which is correct.

*You can also subscript characters, e.g. H₂O by clicking **x₂**. Other icons in the Home/Font group let you change the colour of text, etc. Explore the various options.*

What you learned:

- **How to create a superscripted character.**
- *How to subscript a character.*
- *How to change the colour of characters, etc.*

6.3 Numbering and bullets

Highlight part or all of the two paragraphs following *Introduction*. Remember that a new paragraph started when you pressed RETURN.

Click $\equiv$ (*Home/Paragraph - Numbering*). The paragraphs become automatically numbered:

1. *Are you just starting with a computer to write letters?*

2. *Have you been using a word processor for some time but still find it intimidating and feel that you don't understand what it's doing?*

Click ▾ next to $\equiv$. A box appears. Click on an alternative numbering style, e.g. *a) b) c)*. The numbers are changed to letters.

You could choose various other numbering styles including Roman numerals.

With the two paragraphs still selected, click $\stackrel{\text{\tiny 1}}{\underset{\text{\tiny 3}}{\equiv}}$ repeatedly. The letters appear and disappear. Leave them on.

Place the text cursor just after *doing?* and press RETURN:

a)   *Are you just starting with a computer to write letters?*

b)   *Have you been using a word processor for some time but still find it intimidating and feel that you don't understand what it's doing?*

c)

A letter appears and you could start typing a new lettered paragraph. Press CTRL+Z to undo this and get back to where you were.

Press SHIFT+RETURN. A new line starts and you could type another paragraph relating to item b). When you press RETURN again, item c) would open.

Press CTRL+Z to get back to where you were. Press RETURN, then BACKSPACE. The list is ended. You could start typing normal paragraphs with the same indentation as items in the list.

Press BACKSPACE again. You could start typing normal paragraphs with the same indentation as the numbers or letters of the list.

Press BACKSPACE again. You could start typing unindented paragraphs.

Press BACKSPACE a fourth time. It's as if you'd never pressed RETURN.

This is confusing and you'll probably not remember how many times to press BACKSPACE. Just try to remember SHIFT+RETURN starts a new line in the current list item, pressing BACKSPACE a few times exits the list with different indentation and that, if you press BACKSPACE enough times, you can get rid of the last RETURN.

You can change list entries to a different level (e.g. change paragraphs 2 and 3 in a list so they are numbered as 1.1 and 1.2 instead). Highlight the paragraphs you want to change and click $\stackrel{\text{\tiny 1}}{\underset{\text{\tiny ?}}{\equiv}}$ (Home/Paragraph – Multilevel List). A box appears where you can choose a multilevel format, e.g. 1, 1.1, 1.1.1. Click $\rightleftarrows$ Change List Level near the bottom of the box. Another box *appears where you can click to choose the level of the selected paragraphs, e.g. 1.1 to demote them from 2 and 3 to 1.1 and 1.2. You may need to experiment a bit.*

Select the two paragraphs again and click on the bullets icon (⠿≡). The numbers change to dots (**bullets**):

- *Are you just starting with a computer to write letters?*

- *Have you been using a word processor for some time but still feel that it's intimidating and you don't understand what it's doing?*

What you learned:

- **How to create a list of numbered or lettered items.**

- **How to add an item to the list.**

- **How to start a new line in an existing list item without it becoming a new list item.**

- **How to end the list with different indents.**

- **How to change the numbering style, e.g. to Roman numerals.**

- **What a bullet is and how to create a list with them.**

- *How to create a multilevel numbered list.*

6.4 Formatting paragraphs

Click to position the text cursor anywhere in the first line (*Introduction*).

On the ribbon under *Home/Styles,* you should see a style selector box with various paragraph styles, starting with *Normal.* There should be an outline around Normal: this is because *Introduction* (like all of the document) is currently formatted in the Normal style.

If the box isn't visible (because your window or screen is too small), you'll see A⩘ Quick Styles instead. Click on it. A larger box appears showing the various styles.

Remember that some icons like the Quick Styles one here are rearranged to fit better.

Look for the style labelled *Heading 1* and click on it. The whole line is given a different paragraph style suitable for a chapter title. Its typeface, style and size changes.

You might have to click ▼ next to the box to get to Heading 1.

When you move the mouse cursor over a style in the box, selected paragraphs temporarily change to that style. Don't be alarmed: this is only a preview. The document isn't changed unless you click on a style.

Position the text cursor on the blank line above *Basics of Windows* and press DELETE.

We put a blank line to make it easier to spot the new chapter. It won't be needed any more.

Make sure the cursor is on *Basics of Windows*. Click on *Heading 1* in the paragraph styles selector box. The line changes to a chapter title like *Introduction*.

Position the cursor in the line that reads *Clicking with the mouse* and click *Heading 2* in the style selector box. The line is given a style suitable for a subsection of a chapter. Repeat this with the line that reads *Starting the Web browser*.

Again, you might have to click ▼ next to the box to get to Heading 2.

What you learned:

- **That all paragraphs in a document are initially in Word's *Normal* style**
- **How to change individual paragraphs such as chapter titles to a different preset style.**

6.5 Modifying a paragraph style

There isn't much difference between the Heading 1 and Heading 2 styles. We'll soon fix that!

Right-click on *Heading 1* in the style selector box and click on ⅄ Modify... in the box that appears. The *Modify Style* dialogue box opens.

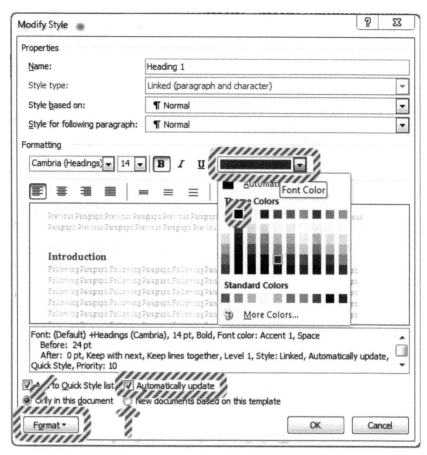

We don't really want the chapter headings to be in blue: that'll only make the document harder to print and photocopy. Click the font colour box (circled). A selector box appears as shown. Click the black square (circled). The headings change to black.

Click the *Automatically update* tickbox (circled) so it's ticked as shown.

Click on the circle to the left of *Only in this document* (arrowed) so that it is filled in and the circle to the left of *New documents based on this template* (also arrowed) is cleared as shown.

> *If New documents based on this template was filled in instead, the changes you're making to the paragraph style would affect the Normal.dot template used for future blank documents.*

*The circles are known as **Radio buttons**. Like the station buttons on a car radio and unlike tickboxes (Section 4.5), only one can be selected at a time – the previous choice is automatically cleared.*

Click [Format ▾] (circled) and click *Paragraph...* in the list that appears. The Paragraph style dialogue box appears.

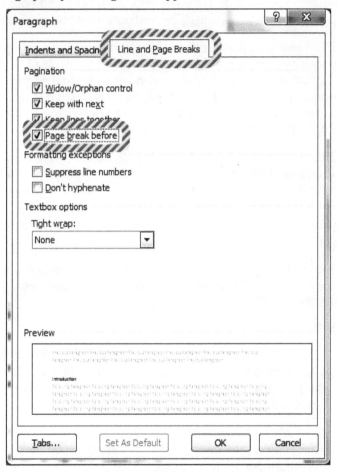

Click the *Line and Page Breaks* tab (circled). Click the *Page break before* tickbox so it's ticked as shown. Click [OK] and click [OK] again to close the *Modify Style* box.

Each chapter now starts on a new page. Depending on the current view mode you may only see a dashed line marking the start of each page.

You can change the mode in View/Document Views on the ribbon. Click 🔲 Print Layout *to see the pages as they will be printed. You may find it easier to work in* ▤ Draft *layout.*

Drag or triple-click to select either of the chapter headings in the document (*Introduction* or *Basics of Windows*). Change the font size to *20* as in Section 4.9. Click ≡ (*Home/Paragraph*). Note that both chapter headings change: this is because you ticked *Automatically update.*

When you set a paragraph to use a particular style, this doesn't prevent you from making other changes to the style of individual characters or words or even making changes to the style of the whole paragraph, e.g. by changing its justification. Unless the assigned style has Automatically update ticked, the changes won't affect other paragraphs using the same style.

This can cause problems: a paragraph may look odd or behave strangely in the table of contents because of some local formatting that you've forgotten about. You can remove all local formatting of a paragraph by selecting all of it, clicking 🔡 *(Home/Font – Clear Formatting), then clicking the required paragraph style again.*

You'll often want to make tweaks to individual paragraphs of body text. The Normal style doesn't let you choose Automatically update.

What you learned:

- **How to adjust one of Word's preset paragraph styles.**
- **That a change to a paragraph style immediately affects all the paragraphs of that style in the document. You don't have to find them all and change them one by one.**
- **What Automatically update does.**
- *That you can still change the formatting of text and individual paragraphs.*
- *How to remove any formatting of an individual paragraph.*
- *That you can make your changes to a paragraph style apply to all new documents or only to the current one.*
- *What Radio buttons are and how they differ from tickboxes.*
- *That different screen layouts for your document can be selected at View/Document Views.*

6.6 Numbering the chapters and sections

Make sure the text cursor is still in one of the chapter headings. Click ⁱₐ⁼ₜ (*Home/Paragraph* – *Multilevel List*). Click Define New Multilevel List.... The *Define new Multilevel List* dialogue box opens. Click More >> .

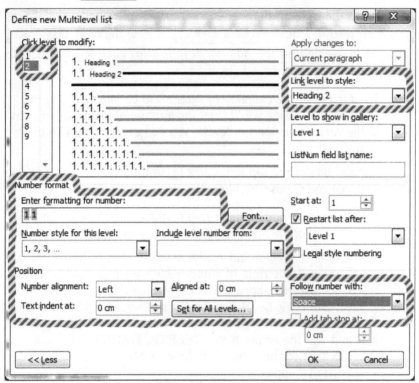

> *You can have up to 9 levels of numbering: we'll only be using two of them (Chapters and Sections).*

Click *1* in the box at the top left (circled). Click ▾ to the right of *Link level to style:* (circled) and choose *Heading 1*.

> *You've just told Word that paragraphs using the Heading 1 style are to be at the top level of the numbering scheme, i.e. the chapter names.*

You need to adjust several of the circled *Number format* and *Position* boxes. Click ▾ to the right of *Number style for this level:* and click on *1, 2, 3* in the list that appears. Check that the *Enter formatting for number:* box just above shows only the number *1* – you can click in it and use the arrow keys and DELETE or BACKSPACE to get rid of anything else. Click ▾ to the right of *Follow number with:* and click on *Space* in the list that appears.

> *This tells Word to put a number (1, 2, 3, etc.) followed by a space before each chapter heading.*

Click ▾ to the right of the the *Aligned at:* and *Text indent at:* boxes until both read *0*. Click ‎ Set for All Levels... ‎. A new dialogue box opens. Click ▾ to the right of the *Additional indent for each level:* box until it also reads *0*. Click ‎ OK ‎.

> *We don't want the chapters or sections to be indented. In other types of documents, you'll want indentation of headings and text at the various numbering levels: you can experiment with the settings.*

Click *2* in the box at the top left. Click ▾ to the right of *Link level to style:* (circled) and choose *Heading 2*.

> *Paragraphs formatted in the Heading 2 style will be at the second level of the numbering scheme (sections).*

The circled *Number format* and *Position* boxes need to be set for this level too. Click ▾ to the right of *Number style for this level:* and click on *1, 2, 3* in the list that appears. Click ▾ to the right of *Include level number from:* and click *Level 1* in the list that appears. Check that the *Enter formatting for number:* box just above shows only 1.1 – you can click in it and use the arrow keys, DELETE, BACKSPACE and . to correct it. Click ▾ to the right of *Follow number with:* and click on *Space* in the list that appears.

> *This tells Word to put the chapter number and a dot followed by the section number and a space before each section heading.*

Click ‎ OK ‎ to close the *Define new Multilevel list* dialogue box. Scroll through the document. You'll see that the chapters and sections are numbered. The section numbers include the chapter number too.

> *If you see that you made an error in setting up the list, position the text cursor in any chapter or section heading, click ⁱↄ and click Define New Multilevel List.... Confusingly, this now doesn't define a new list at all: it reopens the dialogue box for the existing list. Make the changes you want and click ‎ OK ‎.*

Oops, we missed a chapter!

Position the cursor on the blank line above *Behind the screen* and press DELETE. Make sure the cursor is on *Behind the screen*. Click on *Heading 1* in the paragraph styles selector box (Home/Styles).

The line becomes the title for Chapter 2. *Basics of Windows* and its sections are automatically renumbered as Chapter 3.

What you learned:

- **How to use a multilevel list to number chapters and sections.**

- **That the numbers update automatically when you make changes to the document.**

- *That you can automatically indent the headings and associated text.*

- *How to reopen the Define new Multilevel list dialogue box when you need to make changes.*

6.7 Inserting a table

In Section 4.7 you saw how tab stops can be used to line up text in columns. You could use this to type a table in your document but Word has an easier way.

Click at the end of the last line in Chapter 1 (*If you fit either description, this book is meant for you.*) and press RETURN.

Click ⊞ Table (*Insert/Tables* on the ribbon). A box appears with a lot of squares in it. Move the mouse cursor over the fourth square from the left in the second row from the top. *4x2 Table* appears above. Click. A blank 4 column table is created with the cursor in the top left rectangle.

Type *Program* and press TAB. The cursor moves to the next box. Type *Formatting* and press TAB. Type *Styles* in the next box and *Grammar* in the last (top right) box. After you press TAB, the cursor should be in the left hand box on the second row. Type *Notepad* and press TAB.

> *When you're typing in a table, TAB moves to the next box to the right.*

Type *No, No* and *No* in the three boxes to the right of *Notepad*, pressing TAB after each *No*. A new blank row appears.

> *Notepad is a simple text editor included with Windows.*

Type *Libreoffice, Yes, Yes* and *No* in the four boxes in the new row.

Type *Word, Yes, Yes* and *Yes* in the four boxes of the next row.

Oops, two problems! You've got another blank row and you should have capitalised the *O* in *LibreOffice*.

You'll see that two new tabs have appeared on the ribbon. These are there whenever the text cursor is in a table. Click the *Layout* tab and click ▓**Delete**. A box appears. Click ⊒ Delete Rows . The unwanted blank row disappears.

Click on *Libreoffice* or use the arrow keys to move to it. Change the *o* to *O*.

Oops again! We forgot about WordPad. Click on *Notepad*. Click ▦ Insert Below (*Layout/Rows & Columns*). A blank row is inserted between *Notepad* and *LibreOffice*. Type *WordPad, Yes, No* and *No* into it.

> *WordPad is a simple word processor that's included with Windows. Although it can open and save Word documents, it lacks many features and can't display or modify complex documents correctly.*

Move the mouse cursor outside the table to the left of *Program*. The cursor changes to a large arrow. Click. The whole first row of the table is selected. Click **B** (*Home/Font*) or press CTRL+B. The selected words change to **bold**.

> *You can select single or multiple entries in a table and change their justification, typeface, size and style just like any other text.*

> *The first row of the table shows the column headings. Right-click anywhere in the first row and click ▒ Table Properties... in the list that appears. A dialogue box opens. Click the Row tab, then click the tickbox to the left of Repeat as header row at the top of each page so that it's ticked. Click ⌷ OK ⌷. This makes sure that, if the table won't all fit on one page, the first row will be repeated at the top of the part of the table on the next page.*

> *Drag to select all cells in the table. On the Design tab, you'll see various predefined Table Styles. You can see more styles by clicking ▾ to the right of the styles box. If you see a style you particularly like, click on it. The table is reformatted.*

Alternatively, click on ▾ to the right of ⊞ Borders. A list appears and you can change the style of lines around the selected cells. Choose ⊞ No Border if you don't want any lines at all: this makes the table print out the same as it would if you'd used tab stops to set it up.

Click at the start of *Formatting* at the top left of the table and drag to after *Yes* at the bottom right. All of the last three columns are selected. Click ≡ (*Home/Paragraph*). The text in each selected cell is centred.

If you place the cursor over the line between columns in the table, it changes to a line and arrows pointing side to side. You can drag it to change the width of the columns.

Click below the table. Click **B** or press the CTRL+B shortcut and type *Word Processor features*. Click ≡ to centre the caption.

If you fit either description, this book is meant for you.

Program	Formatting	Styles	Grammar
Notepad	No	No	No
WordPad	Yes	No	No
LibreOffice	Yes	Yes	No
Microsoft Word	Yes	Yes	Yes

Word Processor features

What you learned:

- **How to insert a blank table.**
- **How to type text into the table.**
- **How to delete and insert rows in the table.**
- **How to edit text in the table.**
- **How to format text in the table.**
- *What happens if the table won't fit on the current page.*
- *How to change the style of the lines in the table.*
- *How to adjust the width of the table columns.*

6.8 Adding a table of contents

Place the text cursor before the title of Chapter 1 (*Introduction*). Make sure nothing is highlighted. Click 📄 Table of Contents ▾ (*References/Table of Contents* on the ribbon). A box appears showing several possible types of table.

Click on either of the *Automatic Tables* (the only difference is that one says *Contents*, the other says *Table of Contents*). The table is created though you may need to scroll up to see it. The table shows the chapters and sections in your document, complete with page numbers:

Table of Contents

1   *Introduction*..*1*
2   *Behind the Screen*......................................*2*
3   *Basics of Windows*.....................................*3*
       3.1   *Clicking with the mouse*....................*3*
       3.2   *Starting the Web Browser*.................*3*

You'll notice that the page numbers are wrong. The new index is on page 1 and Introduction is on page 2. We'll fix that in a moment.

You can mark words as entries for an alphabetic index by selecting one of them, clicking ⊟₊ Mark Entry *(References/ Index) or pressing ALT+SHIFT+X, then clicking* [Mark] . *While the dialogue box is open, you can select more words, clicking in Main entry: and pressing* [Mark] *again for each one. Close the dialogue box, click where you want the index to go and click* ⊟ Insert Index *(References/Index). The Index dialogue box opens. Click on the Index tab, choose how many columns you want the index to be formatted in, then click* [OK].

You can set up a cross-reference in your document (e.g. See Page 1234) by clicking where you want the reference to point to. Click 🔖 Bookmark *(Insert/Links). A dialogue box opens. Give the bookmark a name that you'll recognise later, then click* [Add]. *Click where you want the cross-reference to appear and click* 🔲 Cross-reference *(Insert/Links). Choose Bookmark as Reference type: and click to select the bookmark you want. Under Insert reference to:, you can choose what to show: the page it's on or its paragraph number (if it has one) and/or whether it's above or below the cross-reference. Click* [Insert] *to add the cross-reference and click* [Close] *to close the dialogue box.*

The Table of Contents and any index and cross-references don't automatically update when you make changes to the document (e.g. inserting the table of contents itself). They don't even update when you save and reopen it! Press CTRL+A to select everything in the document, then press the F9 key at the top of the keyboard. You're then asked whether to update everything or just the page numbers: you'll probably want to choose everything.

The F1 to F12 keys are known as Function keys. With some keyboards, these keys have other functions too and only work as Function keys when the FN key is pressed or FN LOCK is enabled.

You can also update the table of contents by clicking ▤ Update Table (References/Table of Contents), then click ▤ Update Index (References/Index) to update an index but CTRL+A then F9 is safer because it updates all your references at once.

*You'll notice that ▤ Update Index is shown in grey (**greyed out**) and clicking on it does nothing unless you've created an index and placed the text cursor in it. Unfortunately it's often hard to figure out why some icons or options in a dialogue box are greyed out.*

What you learned:

- **How to create a table of contents.**
- **How quick and easy this is if you use paragraph styles and outline numbering.**
- **How to update the table of contents and any indexes and cross-references.**
- *How to create an index and cross-references.*
- *What the Function keys are.*
- *That icons or options in a dialogue box are sometimes greyed out and cannot be used.*
- *That it may not be easy to figure out why an icon or option is greyed out.*

6.9 Giving the document a title

Click the *File* tab on the ribbon, then click *Info* on the left-hand side. At the right of the main window, you'll see a *Properties* section. Click on Add a title, type *Mini book* and press RETURN.

You can set other information including the document's author. This information, which doesn't appear in the document itself unless you insert it as a field, is known as meta-data.

Under Properties, you see other information about the document including a word count.

What you learned:

- **How to set document meta data, including a title.**
- **How to see statistics about the document, including a word count.**
- *What meta-data is.*

6.10 Adding a footer or header and fields

Click 📄 Footer ▾ (*Insert/Header & Footer*). A box appears with various pre-defined footer styles. Click the first style shown (*Blank*). A header area appears at the top and a footer area appears at the bottom of each page. A *Design* tab appears on the ribbon.

Make sure the text cursor is in a footer. Click 📄 Quick Parts ▾ (*Design/Insert*) and move the mouse cursor over 🔲 Document Property in the list that appears. Another box appears. Click on *Title* in it. The book title (*Mini book*) appears in a small box in the footer.

Press RIGHT ARROW to get out of the box. Press SPACEBAR, press – and press SPACEBAR again. Click 📄 Quick Parts ▾ and click ▤ Field... in the list that appears. The *Field* dialogue box opens. Choose *Links and References* in the *Categories:* box and click on *StyleRef* in the *Field names:* box below. Click *Heading 1* in the *Field properties* box and click [OK]. The chapter name (the last paragraph formatted as *Heading 1*) is shown.

> *When you insert a **field**, it brings in information from somewhere else such as the current chapter name. You can insert fields anywhere in your document by clicking* 📄 Quick Parts ▾ *(Insert/Text).*

Press TAB, then type *Page* and press SPACEBAR. Click ⌗ Page Number ▾ (*Design/Header & Footer*) and move the mouse cursor over ⌗ Current Position ▸ in the box that appears. Another box appears. Click *Plain Number* in it. The current page number appears in the footer.

Press SPACEBAR and type *of*. Press SPACEBAR again. Click
▦ Quick Parts ▾ (*Design/Insert*) and click ▭ Field... in the list that
appears. The Field dialogue box opens again. Choose *Document
Information* in the *Categories:* box and click on *NumPages* in the
Field names: box below. Click ▭ OK ▭. The total number of pages are
shown.

> *If you tick Ruler (View/Show), you'll see that a Centred tab stop
> (⊥) was created automatically so that the page numbers are
> centred in the footer. You can drag ⊥ off the ruler. This puts
> the title at the left side and the page numbers at the right.*

Look through the document. You'll see that there's a footer on each
page, each showing the appropriate chapter name and page number.

> *You can put text and/or fields in the header at the top of each
> page instead of or as well as a footer.*

Click ☒ Close Header and Footer (*Design/Close*). The header and
footer areas may no longer be visible. However, if you click
▤ Print Layout (*View/Document Views*), you'll see the document
pages as they would be printed. Any headers and footers are visible in
grey (but they would print in black).

> *You can reopen the header or footer for editing by clicking
> ▤ Header ▾ or ▤ Footer ▾ (Insert/Header & Footer) and clicking
> ▤ Edit Header or ▤ Edit Footer near the bottom of the box that
> appears.*

> *The sizes of the header and footer depend on what's in them. If
> there isn't anything there, they don't take up any space on the
> page.*

What you learned:

- **How to add headers and footers to every page.**
- **How to insert meta-data such as the document title.**
- **How to use fields to insert information that's calculated or
  updated automatically.**
- **That the header and footer are there all the time but they
  are only visible while you're editing them or while you're
  using Print Layout view.**
- **That, although headers and footers may be grey on the
  screen, they print normally.**

You won't be using the document again but you can save it for posterity if you want.

6.11 Creating a PDF file

If you want to send your document to someone else, you can send it as a **PDF (Portable Document Format)** file. This has advantages:

- The recipient doesn't need to have Word or any other word processor.

- Most computers and even many smartphones already have a PDF viewing program installed and, if not, it's free to download and install.

- The document will appear and print out exactly as you intended, even if the recipient doesn't have the same fonts installed.

- The recipient normally won't be able to edit the document: this could be an advantage or a disadvantage.

To create a PDF file, click the *File* tab, then click *Save & Send* at the left hand side. (Your version of Word might show *Share* instead.) Click ▤ Create PDF/XPS Document, then click ▤ Create PDF/XPS to its right. A dialogue box opens where you can choose the name and folder for the new PDF file and set other options. Click ⌐ Publish ⌐. The file is created.

> *Word knows that you won't be able to edit the PDF file. It may remind you to save the document again as a Word file when you try to quit.*

> *Whether you want to send the document as a PDF file or as a Word file, you can copy the file to a disk or thumbdrive and give it to the recipient or you can attach it to an e-mail and send it to them.*

> *Older versions of Word can't create PDF files without an add-on program.*

What you learned:

- **What a PDF file is and what's needed to open it.**

- **That even many smartphones can be used to view PDF files.**

- **That a document sent as a PDF file will appear exactly as you intended but it cannot be edited.**

- **How to export a document as a PDF file.**

6.12 Saving as a different file type

Click ![icon] Save As on the *File* tab. The *Save As* dialogue box appears. Click ▾ to the right of the *Save as type:* box. A list of different file formats appears.

You can click on one of these formats, set the file name as in Section 4.13 and click [Save]. The document is saved in the specified format.

If you'll be sending the file to someone who only has an old version of Word, they may not be able to open it if it's in the current Word format (*Word Document (*.docx)*). You can choose an older Word format (e.g. *Word 97-2003 Document (*.doc)*) instead.

> *If you're sending the document to an OpenOffice or LibreOffice user, you can save it in OpenDocument format. However, they should have an up-to-date version (it costs them nothing) and be able to open .docx files.*

> *Word can save documents as many other file types.* **Rich Text Format (.rtf)** *files can be opened with almost any word processor but anything more than the simplest text formatting may be lost.* **Plain Text (.txt)** *is the simplest file type of all – it's just an electronic version of the paper tape in Chapter 2. The words in your document are saved but all formatting is lost.*

> *Word can open existing files in a number of formats including OpenDocument and old* **WordPerfect** *files. If the file doesn't open automatically in Word, Section 11.1 shows how to specify which program to use to open it – choose Word rather than Notepad.*

What you learned:

- **How to save your document in an older Word format.**

- *That LibreOffice can open Microsoft Word files.*

- *That Word can save and open documents of many other file types including LibreOffice ones.*

6.13 Templates

If you often make similar documents, for example if you need to write a monthly report, wouldn't it be nice to be able to start a new version with the paragraph styles and header or footer already set up? Not only would this save time, it would also help to keep new versions consistent in style with the previous ones.

When starting a new version, you could open a previous version, delete all the text that's not going to be needed in the new version, click ⬛ Save As on the *File* tab to set the file name for the new version, then start typing the new text. This means having to delete a lot of stuff every time you start a new version of the document and there's the risk that you'll forget to rename it and lose the old version when you save the new one.

The better way is, after saving the document, to delete everything that won't be needed in future versions, then save it again as a **template** file. Click ⬛ Save As on the *File* tab and choose *Word Template* under *Save as type:*.

Windows knows this is a different type of file with a different extension (*.dotx* instead of *.docx*). The existing document file won't be overwritten even if the template file has the same name.

When you want to make a new document based on it, open the template file in exactly the same way as you would open the document file. Windows knows to use Word to open this type of file. Word knows that, when you open a template file, you're starting a new document. When you click 💾 or click 💾 Save on the *File* tab, you'll be asked to give your document file a new name.

> *Word includes pre-made templates that you might find useful, e.g. if you need to write a business letter. To see and choose one of these, click New at the left on the File tab.*

> *If you open a template or other file (by clicking or double-clicking on its icon) but decide that you don't want to use it, you can close it without quitting Word itself by clicking 📄 Close on the File tab.*

What you learned:

- **How to prepare and save a template file.**

- That, when you open a template file, Word knows you are starting a new document and will make sure you give it a name when you save it.
- *That Word comes with templates for various tasks.*
- *How to close a document without quitting Word itself.*

7 Spreadsheets

Did you ever try to add up a column of numbers but got a different answer every time?

A spreadsheet is a powerful tool when you need to work with numbers. Not only does it do complicated calculations in a flash, it does them consistently and it records exactly how you set up the calculations for future reference.

This chapter is an introduction to the Excel 2010 spreadsheet.

Other spreadsheet programs are similar except for the Ribbon interface.

7.1 Starting Excel

As in Section 4.1, click the 🔵 orb, then click in the *Search programs and files* box. Type *excel*, then click *Microsoft Excel 2010* in the list that appears above the box.

The **spreadsheet** opens. It looks a bit like a table with columns and rows of **cells**. You'll notice the column headers: these identify each column with a different letter (*A, B, C...*). The rows are identified with numbers (*1, 2, 3...*). A **cell** can be specified by giving its column letter and row number. E.g. the top left cell is *A1*. Cell *B1* is to its right and cell *A2* is below it.

Click on cell *A1*. Its border is emphasised. Type *Ingredient* and press TAB. Cell *B1* is emphasised. Type *Amount* and press TAB. Cell *C1* is emphasised. Type *Price each* and press TAB. Cell *D1* is emphasised. Type *Cost*.

You might want to look at the screenshot below.

Click on cell *A2* (below *A1*) so its border is highlighted. Type *Flour (kg)* and press RETURN. Cell *A3* is emphasised. Type *Sugar (kg)* and press RETURN. Cell *A4* is highlighted. Type *Eggs*.

TAB moves to the next cell to the right. RETURN moves to the cell below. SHIFT+TAB moves to the next cell to the left and SHIFT+RETURN moves to the cell above.

Type *0.5* in cell *B2*, *0.3* in cell *B3* and *2* in cell B4. Type *1.1* in cell *C2*,

1.8 in cell *C3* and *0.25* in cell *C4*.

Type *=B2*C2* in cell *D2* and press RETURN. *D2* shows *0.55*.

> *A cell can contain text (words), a number or a* **formula**. *A formula starts with = and it can refer to other cells in the spreadsheet. In this case, the formula says to multiply together the numbers in cells B2 and C2 (amount and price), giving 0.55.*

> *A formula can contain numbers. In a formula, * multiplies, / divides and ^ raises to a power. For example, =6*2 would show 12, =6/2 would show 3 and =6^2 would show 36 (6 squared).*

Click on cell *D2* and press CTRL+C. The formula is copied to the clipboard.

Drag the mouse cursor over cells *D3* and *D4*. Both cells are highlighted. Press CTRL+V. The formula is pasted into these cells.

Click in cell *D3*. You can see the formula it contains in the box at the top of the spreadsheet (circled below). It's *=B3*C3* rather than *=B2*C2* and the value of cell *D3* (*0.54*) is different from that of cell *D2*.

> *When you paste a formula into a cell, any cells that it refers to are usually adjusted according to where the cell is relative to the original one. In Section 7.3 you'll see how to set an absolute reference where this doesn't happen.*

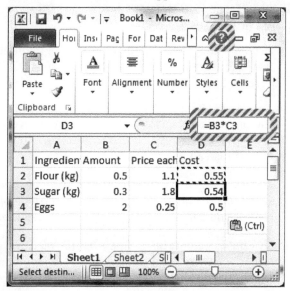

Don't try making this cake. It'd probably be revolting!

What you learned:

- **What a spreadsheet cell is and how it is identified and referenced.**

- **That a cell can contain text, a number or a formula.**

- **That the value calculated by a formula is automatically shown in the cell.**

- **That the formula itself is shown in the box above the spreadsheet.**

- **That a formula can use the values of other cells.**

- **That a formula can be copied and pasted into additional cells.**

- **That, when this is done, any cell references in the formula are adjusted so they are relative to the new cell location.**

- *That you can use numbers as well as cell references in a formula.*

- *How to use TAB, RETURN and SHIFT to move to an adjacent cell.*

7.2 Using functions and inserting rows and columns

Click in cell *B6* and type *SUBTOTAL*. Click in cell *D6* and type *=sum(*. Don't press TAB or RETURN.

Drag the mouse cursor over cells *D2* to *D4*. They are highlighted. Type *)*. You see that the formula in cell *D6* is *=sum(D2:D4)*. Press RETURN. The value in cell *D6* is now *1.59*.

This formula uses Excel's built-in *SUM* function to add the values of cells *D2*, *D4* and any cells in between them. Dragging over these cells automatically puts the **cell range** into the formula. You could have typed it in as *D2:D4* instead.

> *Excel provides many other functions. For example, you can find the minimum, maximum or average value of a range of cells. Mathematical and trigonometric functions are available.*

> *If you click the Formulas tab on the ribbon, you'll see groups of functions in the Function Library section. Clicking on one of these groups shows a list of the available functions. A tooltip*

appears when you move the mouse cursor over a function name:
this gives a brief description of what the function does. Clicking
the function name inserts it into your formula with the = if
required and opens a dialogue box where you can choose the
cell(s) that it refers to.

Click **?** (circled above). A **Help** window opens. Type *sum* into the
Search box near the top and press RETURN. Click on *SUM function* in
the list of topics that appears in the pane. Information about the function is shown.

Microsoft Office, including Word, has a comprehensive though
*not always comprehensible help system. Look for **?** and click it*
for any other questions you have.

The help window is separate from your document. You can resize,
move and minimise it. Click on its ▬ **X** ▬ to close it. Your spreadsheet remains open.

Click cell *B1*. Hold down SHIFT and click cell *D1*. The two cells along
with *C1* are highlighted.

You can select multiple cells in the spreadsheet just like you
select text (Section 4.6) or files in a folder (Section 5.4).

Holding down CTRL lets you add a cell to an existing selection.

Holding down SHIFT and clicking extends the selection by
adding the new cell along with any cells in between.

Click ≡ (*Home/Alignment*). The contents of the selected cells become
centred.

Click on the number *1* to the left of the top row of cells. The whole
row is highlighted.

Click **B** (*Home/Font*). The contents of the highlighted cells are now in
bold.

You can use icons and drop-down lists on the Home tab to
change the typeface, size and style of cell contents, just as in
Word.

Click ⊞ above Insert (*Home/Cells*). A new row of cells is added
above the highlighted one.

If you click on a letter above a column of cells to select it, clicking ⊞ inserts a new column to its left. If you have only one cell selected and click Insert, you can choose whether to insert a row or a column.

Click cell *B2*. Hold down SHIFT and click cell *D7*. All the cells in rows *2-7* of columns *B, C* and *D* (a **rectangular area**) are highlighted. Place the mouse cursor over the dark outline around the selected cells so it changes to four arrows pointing in different directions. Drag the cells one column to the right.

You can insert rows or columns or drag a block of cells to make room for new entries.

References are automatically changed when rows or columns are inserted or cells are dragged. For example, the formula in cell E3 is =C3*D3. It was originally entered as =B2*C2 in cell D2.

What you learned:

- **How to use a built-in function in a formula.**
- **How to use the Microsoft Office Help system.**
- **How to specify a range of cells or select them by dragging.**
- **How to select an entire row or column of cells.**
- **How to change the font (typeface, style and size) used to display cell contents.**
- **How to insert a row of blank cells.**
- **How to select cells in a rectangular area.**
- **How to move selected cells by dragging.**
- ***That Excel has many built-in functions that you can find using Insert > Function....***
- ***That references are automatically changed when you insert rows or drag and drop cells.***

7.3 Column widths and absolute references

Click cell *A1* and type *Cakes per batch*. Click cell *C1* and type *10*.

Click cell *B2*, type *Amount per cake* and press TAB.

Cell C2 is now highlighted. We want to change its contents from

Amount to *Amount per batch*. Click after *Amount* in the box above the spreadsheet that shows the cell contents and press SPACEBAR. Type *per batch* and press RETURN. Cell C2 is updated.

Cakes per batch in cell A1 is shown correctly even though it spills into cell A2. However *Amount per cake* and *Amount per batch* are truncated because the adjacent cells aren't blank. Place the mouse cursor between *B* and *C* above these columns. The cursor changes to a line with two arrows. Drag to the right. Column *B* becomes wider. Widen it enough so that *Amount per cake* is shown properly.

Repeat this procedure to widen column *C* so that *Amount per batch* is shown correctly.

> *You might also need to widen columns A and D slightly.*

Click cell *C3* and drag down to cell *C5*. Cells *C3*, *C4* and *C5* are highlighted. Press CTRL+C. Click on cell *B3* and press CTRL+V. The contents of cells *C3-C5* are copied to cells *B3-B5*.

> *Moving instead of copying these cells would change the references to them in column E. We don't want that to happen.*

Click cell *C3*, type *=c$1*b3* and press RETURN. Click cell *C3* again. Note that the letters *b* and *c* in the formula are automatically changed to *B* and *C* – you don't need to press SHIFT when typing references or function names in a formula.

Press CTRL+C. Highlight cells *C4* and *C5* and press CTRL+V.

> *Note that the values shown in cells C3-C5 are all 10 times larger than the numbers in cells B3-B5.*

If you click on cells C3, C4 and C5 in turn, you'll see that the formulas are *=C$1*B3*, *=C$1*B4* and *=C$1*B5* respectively. The *$* in *C$1* made it an **absolute reference** telling the spreadsheet to always refer to the cell in row *1*, even when the formula is pasted into other cells lower (or higher) in the same column.

> *If you wanted to paste the formula into cells in different columns, you could put $ in front of the letter in the reference. E.g. the formula =C1*B3 would always refer to cell C1 no matter where it was pasted into the spreadsheet.*

What you learned:
- **How to modify the contents of a cell.**
- **How to change the width of a column.**

- **How to specify an absolute reference to another cell that doesn't change when the formula is copied and pasted.**

- **That you don't have to press SHIFT when you type a cell reference.**

7.4 Calculations, currencies and merged cells

Click cell *B9*. Type *Mark-up* and press TAB. Click % (*Home/Number*), type *76* and press TAB twice. Type *=e7*c9* and press RETURN.

> *You've formatted cell C9 as a **percentage** and set it to 76. Excel shows this as 76% and the actual value of the cell becomes 0.76 (76/100).*

Click cell *B10* and type *Batch price*. Click cell *E10* and type = (don't press TAB or RETURN). Click cell *E7*, type + *and* click cell *E9*. The formula shows as *=E7+E9*. Press RETURN.

> *When you're entering or editing cell contents, you can insert a reference to another cell by clicking on it.*

Click on cell *B11* and type *Postage*. Click on cell *E11* and type *5*.

Click on cell *B12* and type *Price per cake*. Click on cell *E12* and type *=e11+e10/c1*. Press RETURN.

Cell E12 shows *7.7984* but that's plainly wrong. The batch price plus postage is just over £30 so the cost per cake should be about £3, not almost £8.

> *It's always a good idea to look at the result of a calculation to see if it looks plausible.*

This error happened because Excel calculates values from formulas using algebraic conventions. Multiplications and divisions are done before additions and subtractions. Excel is dividing the batch price (*E10*) by the number of cakes, then adding the whole postage charge (*E11*). You need to add brackets (parentheses) so that Excel does the addition before the division.

Click on cell *E12*. Click after = in the formula in the box above the spreadsheet and type (. Press the right arrow key repeatedly until the cursor is just before / in the formula. Type) and press RETURN. The price is now 3.2984.

When you're editing cell content, the left and right arrow keys move the cursor backwards and forwards. At other times, they change your position in the spreadsheet.

The costs and prices are a bit of a mess. Surely they should be in pounds and whole pence (or dollars or Euros and whole cents)?

Click on the letter *D* above the third column of cells. The whole column is highlighted. Hold down CTRL and click on the letter *E* at the top of the fourth column. Both columns are now highlighted.

In the *Number* section of the *Home* tab is a box, probably saying *General*. This controls the formatting of numbers in the highlighted cells. Click ▼ to the right of the box and click 🔲 Currency in the list that appears. All numbers in columns *C* and *D* are now formatted as **currency** amounts. The way they appear depends on your location settings: they will usually show the symbol for your local currency and the appropriate number of digits of minor units (e.g. 2 digits for pence or cents).

The price per cake is now shown as £3.30 instead of 3.2984. Excel rounds the amount to the nearest penny.

Click on the number *1* to the left of the top row of cells and click 🔲 above Insert (*Home/Cells*). A new row of cells is added above the highlighted row.

Select the new cells *A1* to *E1*. Click 🔲 Merge & Center ▼ (*Home/Alignment*). Cells *A1* to *E1* are merged into one. Click in the merged cell, type *CAKE PRICE CALCULATION* and press RETURN.

Select cells *B4* to *B6* (e.g. by dragging). Hold down CTRL and select cells D4 to D6. While still holding down CTRL, click on cells *C2*, *C10* and *E12*. You've selected all the cells with numbers (rather than formulas) in them. Release CTRL and click **B** (*Home/Font*).

*Numbers that you might want to twiddle later are now in **bold**.*

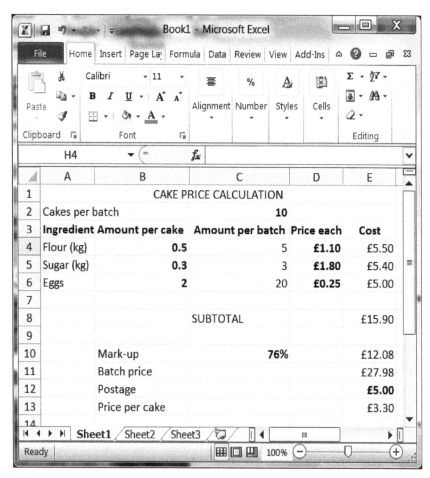

What you learned:

- **What happens when you format a cell as a percentage.**
- **That you can enter a cell reference in a formula by clicking on the cell.**
- **That the order of calculations follows algebraic conventions.**
- **That you can use brackets (parentheses) to change the order of calculations in a formula.**
- **That you can use the left and right arrow keys when you're editing a formula.**
- **That you can add cells to an existing selection by holding down CTRL.**

- **How to format cells so they show their values as currency amounts.**
- **How to merge cells when you need more space.**
- *That you can use the four arrow keys to move around the spreadsheet.*
- *That values are automatically rounded (e.g. to pence) when shown as a currency.*

7.5 Saving the spreadsheet

Click 🖫 at the top left of the window or click the *File* tab and click 🖫 Save As . A dialogue box appears which is similar to the one you see when saving a Word document.

As with Word, type the file name, e.g. *Cakes*. Click | Save |.

> *A spreadsheet can be saved as a template. Choose Save as type: Excel Template.*

What you learned:

- **How to save a spreadsheet file.**
- *That the spreadsheet can be saved as a template.*

7.6 Using the spreadsheet

You can change any of the numbers you formatted in bold and the spreadsheet updates immediately. You can change the number of cakes per batch, the amount or cost of each ingredient, the mark-up percentage or the postage and see the effect.

> *If you change numbers in the spreadsheet just to see what happens, you'll be asked whether to save your changes when you close Excel. Provided that you saved the spreadsheet before you started twiddling the figures and you don't want to save the latest figures you entered, you can click | Don't Save |.*

What you learned:

- **That the whole spreadsheet is updated immediately when you change any value in it.**

8 Charts and Sorting

This chapter covers some more advanced spreadsheet functions including handling dates, sorting rows and making charts (graphs).

The spreadsheet you make in this chapter will also be used in Chapters 9 and 11.

Start Excel. A new spreadsheet opens. Fill in cells *A1* to *C11* with data as follows:

	A	B	C
1	**Title**	**First name**	**Surname**
2	Mr	Riley	Holt
3	Mr	Zachary	Vincent
4	Mrs	Chloe	Vincent
5	Ms	Elise	Gill
6	Mr	Kieran	Kirby
7	Mr	Taylor	Bevan
8	Mrs	Tilly	North
9	Mr	Ellis	Holt
10	Miss	Faith	Bibi
11	Mr	Andrew	Holland

Fill in cells *D1* to *F11* as follows:

	D	E	F
1	**Address**	**Town**	**Postcode**
2	52 Asfordby Rd	ALDBROUGH	DL11 5DL
3	58 Netherpark Cr	STETCHWORTH	CB8 0HZ
4	79 Essex Rd	TARBERT	HS3 4RC
5	92 Gloddaeth St	BIRCHAM TOFTS	PE31 0OR
6	89 Sandyhill Rd	GAER	NP8 3FJ
7	59 Western Tce	MISERDEN	GL6 4OR
8	46 Hindhead Rd	EARDINGTON	WV16 1CO
9	22 Circle Way	CAERAU	CF34 5YN
10	25 Trinity Cr	WHEEDLEMONT	AB54 8HC
11	63 Ivy Lane	WARDGATE	DE6 5II

It's easier to type the town names and postcodes if you press the CAPS LOCK key on the left side of the keyboard first. Remember to press it again afterwards.

Fill in cells *G1* to *I11* as follows:

	G	H	I
1	**Born**	**Height**	**Weight**
2	2/11/40	188	112.1
3	2/4/28	170	88.9
4	9/4/78	156	50.6
5	8/4/81	166	62.4
6	11/8/49	179	109.5
7	9/3/69	170	66.7
8	7/3/43	174	98.4
9	12/5/46	173	84
10	1/6/42	170	59
11	4/12/72	187	87.3

The whole table wouldn't fit in the book: that's why it's in three chunks.

Dates are deliberately chosen so that they appear valid in either American (m/d/y) or European (d/m/y) format. Heights are in centimetres and weights in kilograms.

You might notice that Mr. Vincent is shown as being born in 2028. Leave this as it is.

Press CTRL+A to select all the cells. Click ▦ Format (*Home/Cells*) and click AutoFit Column Width in the box that appears. The widths of the selected columns are set automatically.

Click 🖫 and save the spreadsheet as *People*.

You don't want to have to type all that stuff in again if something goes wrong.

What you learned:

- **That a spreadsheet can be used to make a simple table of data (e.g. names and addresses).**
- **How tedious it can be to type in names and addresses.**
- **How to get Excel to automatically adjust column widths.**

8.1 Making a scatter chart

Are the heights and weights of people in this table related?

Drag to select cells *I4* and *I5*. Put the mouse cursor over the outline and drag the cells to *J4* and *J5*. Select cell *I8*, put the mouse cursor over its outline and drag it to *J8*. Select cell *I10* and drag it to *J10*.

Now the men have their weights in column *I* and the women's weights are in column *J*. Change cell *I1* to *Men* and cell *J1* to *Women*.

Drag to select cells *H1* to *J11*. Click ⋰ Scatter (*Insert/Charts*). A box appears showing different styles of Scatter (X-Y) charts. Click ⋰. A chart (graph) appears, along with three new *Chart Tools* tabs on the ribbon.

Click ⊞ Axis Titles ▾ (on *Layout/Labels* – one of the three new tabs). A box appears below. Move the mouse cursor over ⊞ Primary **H**orizontal Axis Title and click ⊞ **Title Below Axis** in the box that appears.

A box appears in the chart saying *Axis Title*. Type *Height (cm)* – this appears in the box above the spreadsheet. Press RETURN. The axis title is changed.

Click ⊞ Axis Titles ▾ again. This time move the mouse cursor over ⊞ Primary **V**ertical Axis Title and click ⊞ **Rotated Title** in the box that appears. Type *Weight (kg)* and press RETURN.

> *There are three choices for the vertical axis title. Vertical Title places the letters of the title above one another in a column. Horizontal Title places them in a line to the left – this makes the chart quite a bit wider. We've chosen Rotated Title to rotate the line 90 degrees and save space.*

Position the mouse cursor just inside the grey outline around the chart and drag it down and to the left until its top left covers cell *A13*.

Notice that the minimum height is over 150 cm. Right-click on the numbers for the horizontal (Height) axis and choose ⊞ **F**ormat Axis… . A dialogue box opens. Under *Axis Options*, click the circle (radio button) alongside *Fixed* to the right of *Minimum:*. Type *150* into the box just to its right and click [Close].

> *The variation in height is now easier to see.*

The scatter chart is now nicely set up. There's a dot for each person. Its horizontal position shows their height and its vertical position shows their weight. It shows that the men are generally taller than the women and that the taller people tend to be heavier.

Scandal! These people don't really exist. The data you're using is completely fake and has been chosen to make the chart look plausible.

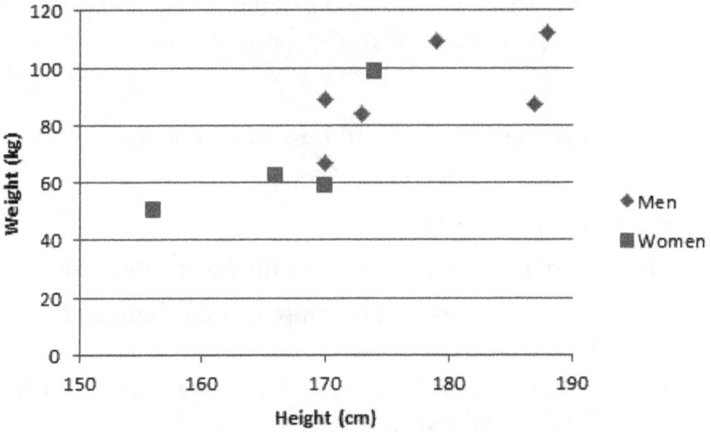

It would be interesting to see these people's *Body Mass Index*.

Click cell *K1* and type *BMI*. Click cell *K2* and type *=10000*i2/h2^2*.

Body Mass Index is the person's weight in kilograms divided by the square of their height in metres. The ^2 tells Excel to square the value of H2. You need to multiply by 10,000 (100^2) because the heights are recorded in centimetres rather than metres.

Copy the formula in cell *K2* into cells *K3-11*.

There's a problem: the women's weights are in a different column and their BMIs are shown as zero. Click on an incorrect cell, then on the formula in the box at the top. Cells in column *H* and *I* are highlighted in different colours, indicating that they are used in the formula. Put the mouse cursor over the outline of the highlighted cell in column *I* and drag it across to column *J*. Press RETURN. The BMI is now correct.

Repeat to fix the BMIs for the other three women.

The BMI values are ridiculously precise. Select cells *K2* to *K11* and click (*Home/Number – Decrease Decimal*) several times. Each time you click it, the number of decimal places decreases by 1. Stop clicking when the BMI values are rounded to one digit after the decimal point, e.g. 30.8 for Mr. Vincent.

Rounding set in Home/Number only affects the values when they are shown. It doesn't affect the results of formulas elsewhere that refer to those cells. E.g. if you enter =K3 as a formula in cell L3 and click ⁺⁰⁰ (Home/Number – Increase Decimal) 5 times, you'll see 30.761246 there. If you wanted to round the value in references to 1 decimal place too, you could use =round(10000*i2/h2^2, 1) as the formula in K2.

What you learned:

- **What a scatter chart is and how to create one.**
- **How to add captions to the chart axes.**
- **How to move the chart.**
- **How to change the minimum value for a chart axis.**
- **That cell references in a formula can be changed by dragging.**
- **How to format cells to show a different number of digits after the decimal point.**
- *That this doesn't affect the value of the cell, only the way it's shown.*
- *That you can use the built-in ROUND() function to round a value in or result of a formula.*

8.2 Date and time calculations

The normal range for BMI is 18.5 to 25. Some of the people are overweight. We'll calculate their ages and see if "middle age spread" is the problem.

Click on the letter K above the eleventh column of cells. The whole column is highlighted. Click ⊞ above Insert (*Home/Cells*). A new column is inserted. Type *Age* into the new blank cell *K1*. Type *=now()-g2* into cell *K2* and press RETURN.

You see a meaningless date in *K2*. With *K2* selected, click ▾ to the right of the box now saying *Date* in the *Number* section of the *Home* tab. Click **12 Number** in the list that appears. The cell shows a huge number which is still pretty meaningless.

Change the formula in cell *K2* to *=int((NOW()-G2)/365.25)* and press

RETURN. Select cell *K2* again and click ⚏ (*Home/Number –
Decrease Decimal*) twice. The cell shows Mr. Holt's age correctly.

*The NOW() function gives the current date and time when the
cell is edited or a saved spreadsheet is opened. The date and
time is in days since the start of 31 December 1899: the
fractional part gives the time of day. For example, midday on 1
January 1900 is represented by the number 1.5.*

*If a cell contains something that looks like a date and/or time,
Excel automatically converts it to a number and formats the cell
so that it interprets the number in a format similar to what you
entered (it may not be exactly the same). When you enter a time
without a date, it's converted to a number between 0 and 1, as if
it was that time on 31 December 1899. When you enter a date
without a time, it's converted to a whole number as if the day
had just started.*

*You can tell Excel to display any number as if it's a date and/or
time of day. If you click ▼ next to the box at Home/Number and
choose More Number Formats... from the list, a dialogue box
opens where you can choose how to show a number, e.g. as a
date or time or as a **fraction**.*

*You can add or subtract cells containing dates and times, e.g. to
see how much time has elapsed between two dates and times or
when some number of days will have elapsed. No need to
account for how many days there are in each month.*

*We want the ages in years rather than days so we need to divide
by the number of days in a year. We're using 365.25 days to
account for leap years.*

*We also want to see the person's age at their last birthday. If
someone is 29 years and 8 months old, we want to see 29, not
29.67 or 30 (which is 29.67 rounded to the nearest whole
number). The INT() function rounds numbers down.*

*The result will still be wrong very occasionally because of our
simplification of leap years.*

*You might input something that Excel thinks is a date or time,
and tries to convert when it shouldn't. For example, suppose you
note the terms of a loan by typing APR 10 into a cell. Excel
interprets this as a date. You can prevent this or other attempts*

to interpret a text string as a number by starting it with a single quote, e.g. 'APR 10.

Copy the formula in cell *K2* into cells *K3-K11* so that everyone's age is shown.

Oops! Mr. Vincent's age is negative!

When you enter a date with a two digit year (e.g. 2/4/28), Excel guesses the century. It normally uses a cut-off year of 1930: years 30-99 are in the 20th century (1930-1999) while years 00-29 are in the 21st century (2000-2029). It thinks Mr. Vincent isn't born yet.

Click cell *G3* and enter the date of birth as *2/4/1928*. His age is now correct.

What you learned:

- **How Excel records, calculates and shows dates and times.**

- **That Excel can't always correctly interpret years entered as two digits.**

- *How to determine the current date and time.*

- *How to round down a calculation result.*

- *How to display any number in the way you want, e.g. as a date, time or fraction.*

- *How to calculate elapsed times or when a time will have elapsed.*

- *How to tell Excel that a string is text and not to try to interpret it.*

8.3 Making a column chart

Select cells *K1* to *L11*. Click ▮▮ Column (*Insert/Charts*) and click ▮▮ under *2-D Column* in the box that appears. A column chart is created. Position the mouse cursor just inside the grey outline of the new chart and drag it down so it's to the right of the scatter chart.

The chart shows the ten people in order with two bars for each person. One indicates their age and the other indicates their BMI. There might be a relationship but it isn't at all clear.

Select cells *A2* to *L11*. Click ⇅ Sort (*Data/Sort & Filter*). A dialogue box appears. Set the *Sort by* box to *Age*. Leave the *Sort On* and *Order* boxes as they are (*Values* and *Smallest to Largest*). Click [OK].

> *Be sure to select all the columns required before sorting data. If you miss some out, they'll be left unchanged and will become associated with the wrong records.*

The selected rows are sorted by increasing age and the chart updates automatically.

> *When you choose a column for sorting, it can contain numeric values or text. Text is sorted alphabetically. For example, you could choose Sort by Surname but there are two people with the surname Holt and two with Vincent. You can click [⁄₂↓ Add Level] and choose First name as the first Then by so that people with the same surname are sorted by their first name.*

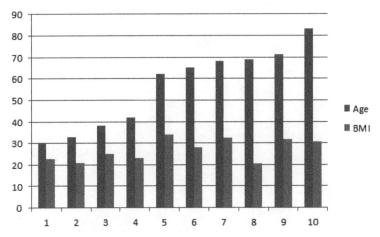

> *The chart shows some slight evidence of middle age spread. A lot more people would have to be added before we could say for sure.*

Be sure to click 💾 to update the saved spreadsheet. You'll be using it again.

> *We've only briefly touched on the different types of chart and the ways to smarten them up. There are a great many options that can be set on the Chart Tools tabs. You may want to experiment.*

What you learned:

- **What a column chart is and how to make one.**

- **How to quickly sort data stored in an Excel spreadsheet.**
- *That you can select a text column to sort data alphabetically.*
- *How to sort on more than one column.*
- *To be careful when selecting the columns to be sorted.*
- *That there's a lot more you can learn about charts.*

9 Graphics and Pages

In this chapter, you'll use Word to write a report based on what you found out in Chapter 8. The report will include the charts from the spreadsheet and will show the raw data as an embedded spreadsheet that looks like a table when it's printed.

This chapter may be most useful to students.

9.1 Pasting graphics and data from the spreadsheet

Start Excel, click the ribbon's *File* tab, then click *Recent*. You'll see the names of recently used Workbooks (spreadsheet files). If *People* (the spreadsheet you made in Chapter 8) is there, click on its name to open it.

> *When you click* 🌐 *and move the mouse cursor over Microsoft Excel, the list of recently used files appears. Just click on the one you want to open it in Excel: that's even quicker and easier.*

If you've used several other spreadsheets since *People*, it may not be listed any longer. You can open it by clicking 📂 Open at the upper left and finding the file or just close Excel, click 🌐, go to *Documents* and open *People*.

> *You can also use the Search programs and files box (Section 3.2) to find and open a document. Type its file name into the box, then click on its name in the list above the box. Sometimes, even typing a word that's in the document itself (though not in its name) will find it.*

Leaving the spreadsheet open, start Word. A new document opens.

Both the new Word document and the People spreadsheet are in your computer's RAM and Word and Excel are multitasking (Section 3.3). You can switch between them by clicking the Word (W) and Excel (X) icons on the taskbar. Switch back to the *People* spreadsheet.

> *You can also switch programs and documents by holding down the ALT key and pressing TAB. The first time you press TAB, you'll see all your open documents and any open folders in a box in the middle of the screen. One of them is highlighted. Each*

time you press TAB again, the highlight moves to the next
document or folder. When it's on the one you want, release ALT.

Click just inside the rectangle around the scatter chart of weight versus height that you made in Section 8.1. It becomes selected (it has a light grey outline). Press CTRL+C to copy it to the clipboard.

Click **W** on the taskbar or use ALT+TAB to switch to the blank Word document. Press CTRL+V and press RETURN. The scatter chart is pasted into the document with the text cursor below it.

Switch back to the *People* spreadsheet, Click just inside the rectangle around the column chart of ages and BMIs that you made in Section 8.3 and copy it to the clipboard.

Switch to the new Word document, make sure that the text cursor is flashing below the scatter chart (click below the chart if it isn't) and press CTRL+V, then press RETURN. The column chart is pasted into the document.

Switch to the *People* spreadsheet. Select cells *B1* to *L11* (a rectangular area) and press CRTL+C to copy it to the clipboard.

Switch to the new Word document, make sure the text cursor is flashing below the column chart and press CTRL+V. The selected cells are pasted into the document as a table. Press RETURN.

What you learned:

- **Two ways to see and quickly open documents you worked on recently.**
- **A situation where it's useful to have two programs running at the same time.**
- **How to paste charts from a spreadsheet into a Word document.**
- **How to paste part of a spreadsheet into a Word document as a table.**
- *That you can find a document by typing its file name or a word that it contains into the Search programs and files box.*
- *How to use ALT+TAB to switch between open documents.*

9.2 Portrait, Landscape and paper size

Click ▢ Print Layout (*View/Document Views*). You'll see that there's a problem: the table is too wide to fit on the page.

Click to the right of the column chart. Click ⊫≣ Breaks ▾ (*Page Layout/Page Setup*) and click ≣ **Next Page** under *Section Breaks* in the box that appears. Make sure the text cursor is on the new page with the table on it, then click ⟮⟯ Orientation (*Page Layout/Page Setup*) and click ≣ Landscape in the box that appears.

Common paper sizes such as A4 (210 x 297 mm) and Letter (8½ x 11 inch) aren't square. Portrait orientation puts the shorter side at the top while landscape orientation puts the longer side there. Think of paintings of a person (portrait) or a scene (landscape) in an art gallery.

You don't need to change the way that the paper is loaded into the printer when you print a landscape page. The computer automatically rotates the image of the page when it sends it to the printer.

If you want to change the whole document to Landscape orientation, you only need to click ⟮⟯ Orientation and ≣ Landscape . Section breaks are needed if you want to have both Portrait and Landscape pages in the same document.

You can click ⟮⟯ Size (Page Layout/Page Setup) and change the page size for your document. Usually, this should match the size of the paper loaded into the printer.

*The **printer driver** installed in Windows to control the printer needs to know the size of the paper. You can set this after clicking Print on the File tab.*

If the document page and printer paper sizes differ, options depend on your particular printer and can't be covered in detail here. Possibilities include:

- *Printing the page normal size with blank space or bits missing.*

- *Shrinking or enlarging the page to fit the paper.*

- *Printing each large page on several smaller sheets of paper that you stick together afterwards (**tiling**).*

- *Printing multiple pages on each sheet of paper, e.g. two A5 portrait pages side by side on an A4 landscape sheet.*

- *Showing an error message or flashing indicator light.*

*Your printer might be able to print on both sides of the paper (**duplex printing**). If not, you can print one side, reload the printed sheets and print the other side: this involves some trial and error.*

The table is now on a second page that's landscape oriented. It's wide enough for the table to fit.

What you learned:

- **How to change the orientation of pages from Portrait to Landscape.**

- *What Portrait and Landscape pages are.*

- *That a section break is needed if you want to mix orientations in the same document.*

- *How to change page and paper sizes.*

- *What might happen if the sizes don't match.*

- *Two ways to print on both sides of the paper.*

9.3 Pasting a spreadsheet

The table we pasted into the new document would be quite adequate but we'll do something a bit more advanced...

Switch back to the *People* spreadsheet, make sure cells *B1* to *L11* are still selected and press CTRL+C.

Switch to the new Word document and click below the table on the second page. Press CTRL+RETURN. A blank page appears.

As mentioned in Section 4.8, CTRL+RETURN inserts a page break. The page break isn't essential here: it's just part of the exercise.

Click **Paste** (*Home/Clipboard* just under) and click Paste Special... in the box that appears. The *Paste Special* dialogue box opens.

You'll see that *HTML Format* is highlighted in the list. Click on *Microsoft Excel Worksheet Object* to highlight it instead. Make sure that the radio button next to *Paste:* on the left is selected, then click

$\boxed{\text{OK}}$. After a short delay, a slightly different second copy of the table appears.

The new copy isn't just a table. Double-click on it. It turns into a little spreadsheet with its own scrollbars (arrowed below) **embedded** in the Word document.

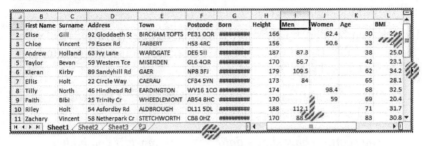

	B	C	D	E	F	G	H	I	J	K	L
1	First Name	Surname	Address	Town	Postcode	Born	Height	Men	Women	Age	BMI
2	Elise	Gill	92 Gloddaeth St	BIRCHAM TOFTS	PE31 0OR	########	166		62.4	30	26.6
3	Chloe	Vincent	79 Essex Rd	TARBERT	HS3 4RC	########	156		50.6	33	
4	Andrew	Holland	63 Ivy Lane	WARDGATE	DE6 5II	########	187	87.3		38	25.0
5	Taylor	Bevan	59 Western Tce	MISERDEN	GL6 4OR	########	170	66.7		42	23.1
6	Kieran	Kirby	89 Sandyhill Rd	GAER	NP8 3FJ	########	179	109.5		62	34.2
7	Ellis	Holt	22 Circle Way	CAERAU	CF34 5YN	########	173	84		65	28.1
8	Tilly	North	46 Hindhead Rd	EARDINGTON	WV16 1CO	########	174		98.4	68	32.5
9	Faith	Bibi	25 Trinity Cr	WHEEDLEMONT	AB54 8HC	########	170		59	69	20.4
10	Riley	Holt	54 Asfordby Rd	ALDBROUGH	DL11 5DL	########	188	112.1		71	31.7
11	Zachary	Vincent	58 Netherpark Cr	STETCHWORTH	CB8 0HZ	########	170	88.5		83	30.8

Sheet1 / Sheet2 / Sheet3

The ribbon changes to the Excel one when the spreadsheet opens. You'll be using the little black squares (circled) in Section 9.8.

When you click [icon] or press CTRL+V, Word pastes whatever is on the clipboard into your document in what it thinks is the way you're most likely to want. The Paste Special dialogue box shows you the different ways that the paste can be done and lets you choose. Unfortunately the names of the different choices can be obscure.

*There are three basic ways something might be pasted. The most advanced and powerful is as an embedded object like this spreadsheet. The second option is as **formatted text** – it looks much as it did where it came from but it may not have all the functions that it originally had. HTML Format is an example of this: it's what Word chose when you pressed CTRL+V and it pasted the spreadsheet cells as a table.*

*The third way is as **unformatted text**. This puts whatever is on the clipboard into the document as if you'd just typed it in, without keeping formatting such as its original font. For example, if you find some useful information on a web page and you want to paste it into a document that's already formatted, you don't want the pasted text to be in the web designer's choice of font.*

When you see the 📋 *(Ctrl)* ▾ *box after you paste something, you can click on it and change the type of paste. The selection may be limited though.*

Change cell *I1* to read *Weight* instead of *Men*. Select cells *J2* and J3 and drag them to *I2* and *I3*. Select cells *J8* and *J9* and drag them to *I8* and *I9*. All the weights are now in column *I*.

Use the embedded spreadsheet's own scrollbar (arrowed) to scroll below the table to the two charts. Click on the left-hand (scatter) one and press DELETE to get rid of it.

Click on the letter *J* above column *J* and click ▦ˣ (*Home/Cells* above Delete). The column disappears.

> *The scatter chart shows data from column J. If you hadn't deleted the chart first, you'd get an error message when you deleted the column.*

> *You can select several columns at once or select rows instead of columns and click* ▦ˣ *to get rid of them.*

> *If you select a cell or range of cells that don't make up a whole row or column, click* Delete *under* ▦ˣ *and click* ⊟ˣ Delete Cells... *in the box that appears, you'll see a dialogue box where you can choose whether to delete just the selected cells and move the cells in all rows below up to fill the space or move the cells in all columns to the right leftwards. You can also choose to delete the rows or columns containing the selected cells entirely.*

> *If you want to delete the cell contents but leave the blank cells in place, you can click* ⌀ Clear ▾ *(Home/Editing), then click* ⌀ Clear All *in the box that appears. You can also delete only certain elements, e.g. formatting such as bold that you've applied to the cells.*

Click on cell *G11* (you may need to use the spreadsheet's scroll bar to see it) and retype the date as *2/4/28*. Press RETURN. Mr. Vincent's age in cell *J11* is negative again. Press CTRL+Z to undo the change.

> *The embedded spreadsheet updates when you change data, just like the original one.*

> *The dates of birth in the spreadsheet might appear to be replaced by ###s. This happens when a spreadsheet column is*

too narrow to show a number. We'll fix that later: meanwhile, you can still type in a different date.

Click to the right of the embedded spreadsheet. It closes: it's now just columns of text, etc.

The headings probably won't be visible and the column widths might need adjustment. We'll fix those soon.

Look at the scatter chart you pasted in at the start of the document. It still shows men and women separately. The chart is just a copy. It's no longer linked to either the People spreadsheet or to the part of it pasted separately into the Word document. It doesn't update.

What you learned:

- **How to start a new page by inserting a page break.**
- **How to embed a spreadsheet into a Word document.**
- **That you can edit the embedded spreadsheet just as if you were using Excel.**
- **That the embedded spreadsheet updates just as if you were using Excel.**
- **How to delete a column from a spreadsheet.**
- **How to close an embedded spreadsheet.**
- *How to delete multiple columns or rows or a range of cells from a spreadsheet.*
- *How to selectively delete the contents of cells, leaving the cells themselves in place.*
- *How to paste text into your document without bringing along its formatting.*
- *That spreadsheet cells and charts pasted separately are no longer linked.*

9.4 Embedding and Linking

You inserted an embedded spreadsheet by copying it to the clipboard and using Paste Special.... There's another way to insert objects such as a spreadsheet or a bitmap image.

Click *Object (Insert/Text). A dialogue box opens with two tabs.*

You can choose an object type on the Create New tab and edit it in your document using the tools of the program associated with it. For example, you can insert a blank Excel spreadsheet which, when it's closed, looks like a list or table in the document. This could be handy if, for example, you're preparing an invoice. Let the spreadsheet do the arithmetic.

Alternatively, you can choose an existing file on the Create from File tab. This makes a copy of the existing file that becomes part of the document and is saved in its file.

If you tick the Link to file tickbox, your document is linked to the specified file instead of containing a copy of it. The document updates when the linked file changes. For example you could record sales in a spreadsheet and make several different reports linked to its file. Updating the spreadsheet updates the reports too but if you e-mail a report file to someone else, you need to send the spreadsheet file as well.

What you learned:

- *What an object is.*
- *That you can insert a new spreadsheet or other object into a Word document.*
- *That you can insert a copy of an existing file such as a spreadsheet.*
- *That you can link to an existing file so that changes to it automatically appear in your document.*

9.5 Inserting pictures

Switch to the *People* spreadsheet. Hold down the ALT key and press the small key marked *Print Scrn*. It's usually near the top right of the keyboard and may have a slightly different label. A screenshot is made of the whole spreadsheet window and it's put on the clipboard.

Pressing ALT+Print Scrn copies the current window to the clipboard. Pressing Print Scrn on its own copies the whole screen, including all visible windows and the taskbar.

Switch to the new Word document, click to the right of the embedded spreadsheet and press CTRL+V. The screenshot appears.

The screenshot is a picture: it's as if you'd used a digital camera to photograph your computer's screen. Instead of pasting, you could click ▨ Picture *(Insert/Illustrations) and choose any picture (e.g. a photograph) that's stored on your computer.*

Instead of pasting the screenshot directly into your document, you could start a picture editing program such as Paint (included with Windows) and paste it there. Then you could make changes such as cropping it to remove bits you don't want or adding circles around things as you've seen in this book. You can either save it as a file and use ▨ Picture *or copy it back to the clipboard and paste it into your document.*

Paint is a very simple program without many facilities. You can buy much better programs such as Adobe Photoshop or you can try the free open-source GIMP. Type GIMP into a search engine, find the Windows version and download and install it. Unfortunately GIMP, although very powerful, can't be described as user-friendly.

Click on the screenshot and press BACKSPACE. It disappears. You saw how to insert the picture but we don't want it.

▨Picture *puts a copy of the picture into your document. Moving, changing or deleting the original file doesn't affect the copy. Removing the picture from the document deletes the copy but doesn't affect the original file.*

Click on the table above the embedded spreadsheet and click ▦ Delete *Layout/Rows & Columns).* Click ▦ Delete Table in the box that appears. The table disappears: we don't want that either.

If you tried to use BACKSPACE or DELETE to get rid of the table, it would only affect letters in it. Even if you select all the text in the table and press DELETE, the empty table remains.

There's now an unwanted blank page. Click ¶ (*Home/Paragraph*) if needed to make non-printing characters visible. Look for the line saying *Page Break*. Place the mouse cursor to its left and click so it's highlighted. Press DELETE.

You can get rid of a section break the same way. Sometimes you may need to insert one or two RETURNs in front of it first so it's on a separate line.

What you learned:

- How to copy a screenshot to the clipboard.
- How to paste a screenshot into a Word document.
- How to remove a screenshot or picture from the document.
- How to delete a table in the document.
- How to remove a page break.
- *How to remove a section break.*
- *How to insert a picture or photograph on your computer into the document.*
- *That inserting a picture or photograph makes a new copy that's part of the document.*
- *That you can edit screenshots or other pictures before you put them in your document.*
- *That you can use Paint to do this but other programs are more powerful.*
- *How to find, download and install an open-source Windows program.*

9.6 Formulas and Equations

You might need to put a mathematical formula or equation into a document, e.g. $\dfrac{-b \pm \sqrt{b^2 - 4ac}}{2a}$. Click π Equation (*Insert/Symbols*), type the equation into the box that appears and press RETURN. Word automatically formats it.

For example, the quadratic formula above can be typed in as *(-b+-\sqrt(b^2-4ac))/2a*.

9.7 Sizing and anchoring graphics

Click 🖻 Print Layout (*View/Document Views*) and click to the right of the scatter chart on the first page.

Make sure *Normal* is selected in the Styles section of the Home tab. Type (pressing RETURN each time you see ¶):

What shape are you?¶

¶
I compared the height and weight of ten people. This chart shows what I found.¶
The women are generally shorter although the taller women are taller than the shortest men.¶
Taller people, both women and men, generally weigh more than shorter ones.¶
¶
This chart shows the age and Body Mass Index of the ten people.¶
There's very little sign here that Body Mass Index varies with age.

Click on the column chart of Age and BMI. A light grey outline appears around it. Place the mouse cursor over the four small dots in the middle of the bottom of the outline. It changes to a double-headed arrow. Drag it upwards. The chart gets shorter but it becomes squashed.

Press CTRL+Z to restore it.

> *Due to a bug in Word, the chart itself may remain squashed when the outline is restored. Ignore this.*

Place the mouse cursor over the bottom right corner of the outline so it again changes to a double-headed arrow. Hold down SHIFT and drag it inwards. The chart shortens and gets narrower in proportion so that its shape is retained. Drag until the chart is about three-quarters of its original size.

> *You can drag any corner or the dots in the middle of any side to move that side or corner. Dragging a corner handle while pressing SHIFT moves the two adjacent sides, keeping the overall width and height in proportion.*

Click on the scatter chart above it, hold down SHIFT and drag the bottom right corner inwards until it's about the same width as the column chart.

Click 🖼 **Position** (*Page Layout/Arrange*) and click 🖼 under *With Text Wrapping* in the box that appears. The chart moves to the top right of the page with some of the text to its left.

> *Charts, pictures, drawings and embedded spreadsheets are all classed as **graphics**. Wrapping controls how text on the page appears around a graphic.*

The wrapping is set to Square. Clicking Wrap Text ▾ *(Page Layout/Arrange) lets you choose other options including:*

- *In Line with Text: the graphic is like a character in the text (rather than being somewhere to the side of it). If the graphic is higher than other characters in the line of text, the spacing of the lines increases to allow it to fit. Small graphics such as* *can be placed in line. A larger graphic can be put in its own paragraph so it sits on the page without any text alongside it.*

- *Square: text fits in alongside the graphic, which needs be placed on the left or right side. If you put it in the middle, you'll get text on both sides which isn't normally what you'd want.*

- *Tight: For a picture, this is generally the same as Square. A drawing such as a logo might not be square, e.g. it might be a circle or a triangle. In that case, Tight allows the text to follow the actual shape of the drawing rather than its rectangular container.*

- *Behind text: Text is placed as if the graphic wasn't there, then the graphic is placed behind it. This can be used to set a light-coloured logo or a word such as DRAFT as a background.*

- *In Front of Text: Text is placed as if the graphic wasn't there, then the graphic is placed over the text. Text behind it is hidden unless the graphic has transparent areas.*

Click ¶ (*Home/Paragraph*) if needed so that non-printing characters are shown.

What·shape·are·you?¶

¶

I·compared·the·height·and·weight·of· ten·people.·This·chart·shows·what·I· found.¶

The·women·are·generally·shorter· although·the·taller·women·are·taller· than·the·shortest·men.¶

Taller·people,·both·women·and·men,· generally·weigh·more·than·shorter·ones.¶

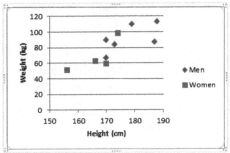

This·chart·shows·the·age·and·Body·Mass·Index·of·the·ten·people.¶

There's·very·little·sign·here·that·Body·Mass·Index·varies·with·age.¶

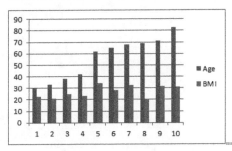

································Section Break (Next Page)································

Note the **anchor** symbol (circled above). Put the mouse cursor just inside the outline around the scatter chart. It changes to four arrows pointing in different directions. Drag the chart downwards. The anchor symbol moves with it. Stop dragging when the anchor is to the left of *I compared*.

This can be temperamental. If the chart ends up lower down the page, drag it up so the anchor's in the right place.

Click on the column chart. It's still set to *In Line with Text* wrapping. Click 📊Wrap Text ▾ (*Page Layout/Arrange*) and click 📊 Square. The chart's anchor symbol appears.

Put the mouse cursor just inside the outline around the column chart and drag it upwards until the anchor symbol is alongside *This chart shows*.

Leave the left side of the chart lined up with the left margin.

Click on *What shape are you?*. Select *Heading 1* in the *Styles* section of the *Home* tab. Click ≡ (*Home/Paragraph*). The heading is centred.

Click to put the text cursor just before *Taller people*. Press RETURN several times until *Taller People* is below the scatter chart and its line widens out.

> *Notice that the column chart moves down, remaining alongside This chart shows the age. It's anchored to that paragraph.*

Click ¶ (*Home/Paragraph*) to hide the non-printing character markers. Page 1 now looks good.

What shape are you?

I compared the height and weight of ten people. This chart shows what I found.

The women are generally shorter although the taller women are taller than the shortest men.

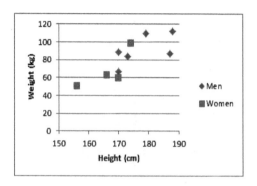

Taller people, both women and men, generally weigh more than shorter ones.

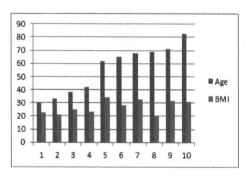

This chart shows the age and Body Mass Index of the ten people.

There's very little sign here that Body Mass Index varies with age.

What you learned:

- **How to change the size of a chart or other graphic.**
- **How to keep the height and width of a graphic in proportion when you resize it.**

- **How to set the text wrapping option so that text appears alongside a graphic.**

- **How to anchor a graphic to a specific paragraph so it moves with it when you make changes.**

- *What is meant by a "graphic".*

- *What the various options are for how text wraps around a graphic.*

- *How to insert a small graphic so it appears in your text just like a character.*

9.8 Adjusting the embedded spreadsheet

Click below the embedded spreadsheet on page 2, then press LEFT ARROW so the text cursor is just to the left of the spreadsheet. Type *The 10 people* and press RETURN.

Click on *The 10 people*. Select *Heading 1* in the Styles section of the Home tab and click ≡ (*Home/Paragraph*).

You may have trouble seeing all of the embedded spreadsheet. Click 📰 Page Width (*View/Zoom*).

> *There are other zoom options. For example, you can choose to see the entire page at once but the text will probably be too small to read.*

Click on the embedded spreadsheet, then click ≡ (*Home/Paragraph*). Double-click the spreadsheet to open it.

Use the spreadsheet scrollbars (arrowed in the Section 9.3 screenshot) to put the top left cell that needs to be visible in the top left of the window. It's cell *B1* in this case. Adjust the width of the columns if needed so the data in each one is visible without too much extra space. Use the black square handles (two of them are circled in the screenshot) to resize the window so you can see all the cells that you want to be visible without unwanted blank rows or columns.

> *Remember: you change the width of a spreadsheet column by placing the mouse cursor between the letters at the top and dragging.*

> *The embedded spreadsheet can be any size but only the cells that are visible in the window when it's open will be visible in the document when it's closed.*

Click outside the spreadsheet to close it. Now page 2 is the way we want it.

Close the new document. You won't be using it again but you can save it for posterity if you want. You can also close the *People* spreadsheet, discarding any changes.

What you learned:

- **Another way to zoom to see more or less of the page at a time on the screen.**

- **How to choose which cells in an embedded spreadsheet are visible.**

10 Drawing and Columns

If you need to lay out a magazine or newspaper, you can use a desktop publishing (DTP) program. Microsoft Publisher is a well-known DTP program suitable for everyday use. Scribus is a free open-source program which is quite capable but perhaps not as user-friendly as its commercial rivals. Professional publishers use very powerful and expensive DTP programs.

Word has DTP capabilities too. This chapter shows how to use it to make a simple newsletter. It also uses Word Picture to create and embed a simple logo.

10.1 Setting up columns

Click 🪟 and go to *Documents*. Open the *WP files* folder and open *LazyDog* (the Word document you made in Chapter 4).

Press CTRL+A to select all the text and CTRL+C to copy it to the clipboard.

Click the ribbon's *File* tab. Click *New* on the left hand side, then click or double-click *Blank Document* under *Available Templates*. A new blank Word document opens. Press CTRL+V. The drivel about the fox and the dog is pasted into it.

> *In Chapter 9 you had a Word document and an Excel spreadsheet open at the same time. Now, you have two Word documents open at once. If you need to switch between them, use ALT+TAB or click* ⬚ Switch Windows ▾ *(View/Window) and choose from the list that appears.*

> *You can also switch between the documents by moving the mouse cursor over* W *on the taskbar. A box appears showing the two Word documents. Click on the one you want.*

Drag over the first three paragraphs of text to select them. Click ▦ Columns *(Page Layout/Page Setup)* and click ▦ Two in the list that appears. The selected text is now in two columns. Click ≡ *(Home/Paragraph)* to fully justify it.

Click 🗔 Shapes *(Insert/Illustrations)* and click ＼ under *Lines* in the box that appears.

Position the mouse cursor at the left margin just below the three paragraphs. Hold down SHIFT and drag across to the right-hand margin. A line appears.

Holding down SHIFT makes sure that it's exactly horizontal.

Place the mouse cursor over the line so that it changes to four arrows pointing in different directions. Right-click and select ✏️ Format Shape…. A dialogue box appears. Click on *Line Style* at the left side. Click ▲ several times to set Width to *1.5 pt*. Click [Close].

You can change many things about the line in the dialogue box, including its colour. You can insert many different shapes too such as rectangles, circles, arrows and stars by clicking 📦 Shapes.

What you learned:

- **That you can start a new document by clicking the *File* tab, then clicking New.**
- **How to put selected text in columns.**
- **How to draw, position and format a separator line.**
- *Three ways to switch between two open Word documents.*
- *How to insert other shapes.*

10.2 Making a logo

This uses the drawing tools to create a new logo. If you already had a logo as a file on your computer, you could use 🖼️ Picture (Insert/Illustrations) as discussed in Section 9.5.

*Computers work with two different types of pictures and drawings. A **bit-mapped** picture specifies the brightness and colour of each point in it. It can show anything: photographs are always bit-mapped. If you try to enlarge a bit-map too much, its individual points become visible as squares and it looks bad.*

*A **vector graphic** contains instructions to draw shapes, colour them in and overlay them. It's limited in what it can show but* *has the advantage that you can easily move and change individual shapes and you can enlarge the graphic to any size.*

Paint works with bit-mapped pictures. The Word drawing tools you'll use here create vector graphics.

Click before the first paragraph to place the text cursor there. Click ⬚ Shapes (*Insert/Illustrations*) and click 🖐 New Drawing Canvas at the bottom of the box that appears. A **Drawing Canvas** (a blank rectangular box with a light grey outline) appears in the document and a new *Format* tab appears on the ribbon..

Click ○ in the box at *Format/Insert Shapes*. Place the mouse cursor at the centre of the drawing canvas, hold down SHIFT and CTRL and drag outwards. A circle appears and grows. Stop dragging when it's almost the height of the drawing canvas.

Holding down SHIFT ensures that you draw a circle (with the same height and width) rather than an ellipse. Holding down CTRL ensures that the circle is centred at the point where you started dragging outwards.

Click ✍ Shape Fill ▾ (*Format/Shape Styles*) and click the yellow square under *Standard Colors* in the box that appears. Click 🖊 Shape Outline ▾ (*Format/Shape Styles*) and click ⬚ No Outline in the box that appears. The circle is now plain yellow.

*Vector graphic shapes have a **fill** and a **stroke**. The fill is the colour inside the shape while the stroke is the line around it. You've set the fill to yellow and made the stroke (outline) invisible. Sometimes you may want to set the fill to none and just use the stroke. Sometimes, you'll want to use both.*

When you're changing the fill colour and you move the mouse cursor over a possible colour, you'll see a tooltip naming it.

Click in the drawing canvas away from the circle so it's no longer selected. Click ▤ Draw Text Box (*Format/Insert Shapes*). Place the mouse cursor in the middle of the yellow circle, hold down CTRL and drag to the left and slightly downwards. A rectangular text box appears and grows. Drag until it's almost the width of the drawing canvas and about the right height to hold a line of text.

There should be a flashing text cursor in the box: if there isn't, click inside it. Type *Sunnyside News*.

Drag to highlight *Sunnyside News*. Click 🅰 Text Effects ▾

(*Format/WordArt Styles*) and move the mouse cursor over ⚶ Transform ▸ in the box that appears. Click ᵒᶜᵈᵉ⸝ (*Arch Up* tooltip) in the box that appears.

Click ⒶText Effects ▾ again and move the mouse cursor over ⒶShadow ▸. Click Ⓐ (*Offset Top* tooltip).

> *WordArt makes it easy to show words with various special effects.*

Click the *Home* tab. You can drag over the text to select it and format it as in Chapter 4. Set it to *26* point *Cambria* and click **B** and ☰.

The text box has a small circle at each corner and a small square in the middle of each side. These are **handles**. Drag the square in the middle of the top upwards and the one in the middle of the bottom downwards until the text box covers the yellow circle.

> *Most graphic objects have handles. You see them when the object is selected and can drag them to resize the object.*

> *There's a small green circle above the top middle handle. Dragging this rotates the object.*

> *You can move an object by placing the mouse cursor over its outline away from any handles and dragging.*

Click ⬧ Shape Fill ▾ (*Format/Shape Styles*) and click No Fill in the box that appears. Click ✏ Shape Outline ▾ (*Format/Shape Styles*) and click No Outline in the box that appears.

> *This makes the text box itself transparent (invisible): only the text in it can be seen across the yellow circle. You can see the effect in the screenshot at the end of this chapter.*

Click ⬛ Send Backward ▾ (*Format/Arrange*). The text moves behind the yellow circle and can't be seen. Click ⬛ Bring Forward ▾ to bring it back to the front.

> *If you have more than two overlapping objects, you can use ⬛ Bring Forward ▾ and ⬛ Send Backward ▾ to stack them in front of one another in any order you want.*

Click on the light grey outline around the drawing canvas. Click 🖻 Position (*Format/Arrange*) and click 🖻 under *With Text Wrapping*. The logo is positioned above the left hand text column.

A Drawing Canvas can be resized and moved and has the same wrapping options as the charts in Chapter 9.

You can use copy and paste to copy the drawing canvas and logo to another Word document. Clicking in the middle of the logo shows the light grey outline but may only select one of the objects: click again on the outline to make sure the whole logo is selected.

It isn't absolutely necessary to use a drawing canvas. You could have drawn the logo directly on the page just like the line you added earlier but it would be harder to position it on the page and to copy and paste it into other documents.

What you learned:

- **How to insert a Drawing Canvas.**
- **How to draw a circle and change its colour.**
- **How to create a Text Box, type text into it and format it.**
- **How to use WordArt to put text on a curve and apply a shadow effect.**
- **What handles are and what they do.**
- **How to make the text box transparent.**
- **What Bring Forward and Send Backward do.**
- *The differences between bit-mapped and vector graphics.*
- *How to use CTRL and SHIFT when drawing.*
- *What Fill and Stroke (Line) are.*
- *What a drawing canvas is.*
- *A way to select the whole of a drawing canvas.*
- *That a drawing canvas can be moved and resized and has wrapping options.*
- *That, once you've made a logo, you can copy and paste it to other documents.*

10.3 Adding a simple text box

Click away from the logo to deselect it. Click A▦ Text Box ▼ (*Insert/Text*) and click *Simple Text Box* in the box that appears.

A text box with handles appears. It contains highlighted text which is replaced as soon as you start typing. Type *January 2012*.

Drag to select *January 2012*. Click the *Home* tab. Change the text to *22* point *Cambria* and click **B** and ☰.

Click ◇ Shape Fill ▾ (*Format/Shape Styles*) and click *Light Green* under Standard Colors in the box that appears.

Place the mouse cursor anywhere over the outline of the text box between handles. The cursor changes to four arrows pointing in different directions. Drag to move the box over the bottom of the yellow circle in the logo.

You can also resize the box slightly by dragging its handles.

You might encounter a bug in Word that prevents you from moving the box correctly. Try dragging it over the right-hand column of text, then moving it from there.

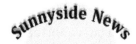

January 2012

The quick brown fox jumps over a lazy dog. **The quick brown fox jumps over the lazy dog.** *The quick brown fox jumps over a lazy dog.* The quick brown fox jumps over the lazy dog. *The quick brown fox jumps over the lazy dog.*

The quick brown fox jumps over a lazy dog. The quick brown fox

jumps over the lazy dog. *The quick brown fox jumps over a lazy dog.* The quick brown fox jumps over the lazy dog. *The quick brown fox jumps over the lazy dog.*

THE QUICK BROWN FOX JUMPS OVER A LAZY DOG. **The quick brown fox jumps over the lazy dog.** *The quick brown fox jumps over a lazy dog.* The quick brown fox jumps over the lazy dog. *The quick brown fox jumps over the lazy dog.*

What do these dogs like?   Walkies   Chasing things

Barking   Eating   Sleeping

If you need to delete a text box, click twice on its edge so that the handles appear but the text isn't highlighted. Press DELETE.

Close the new document. You won't be using it again but you can save it for posterity if you want.

What you learned:

- **How to create a simple text box.**
- **That you can type text into it and format it.**
- **How to change the colour of a text box.**
- **How to resize and move a text box.**
- *How to delete a text box.*

10.4 Making a letterhead

Now that you've seen how to import or create graphics and set up text boxes, you can design your own letterhead.

You can put a logo at the top. Perhaps you already have one that you can insert as a picture or graphic or you could design one using the Word drawing tools.

You can put contact details, perhaps in a text box, at the top or bottom of the page.

You can find sample letterheads by clicking the File tab, clicking on New and clicking the Letterhead folder under Available Templates. Make whatever changes you want: e.g. changing the logo and contact details.

When you're happy with the design, save it as a Word template (Section 6.13). No need to have the letterhead printed, just open the template whenever you start writing a letter.

You need to weigh up the advantages and disadvantages of doing this. A letterhead printed with each letter will print more slowly, will probably be lower quality and may cost more in ink or toner. On the other hand, you'll be sure your letters line up with the letterhead, you won't have to change paper in the printer, there won't be a minimum print run and you can change details on the letterhead (e.g. your phone number) at any time.

11 Mail merge

Mail merge is a word-processor feature that you can use to print personalised versions of a standard letter for people whose names and addresses are in a list somewhere on the computer. You'll have received many of these letters yourself.

Mail merge is an advanced feature but this book covers it since small businesses and organisations will often want to use it.

Before you do a mail-merge, you need to do some planning:

- Where are the names and addresses? Can you get them into Excel or export them as a file that Word can use?

  You saw in Chapter 8 how tedious it is to type a lot of names and addresses. If the names and addresses are in a database, they can probably be exported as a CSV file, perhaps by the database administrator.

- Do you want to send the letter to everyone in the list? If not, is there information in the list itself that can be used to identify who should get a letter?

- Do you want to use windowed envelopes, sticky address labels or print the addresses directly onto envelopes?

  You can buy address labels and run them through the printer. Printing directly onto envelopes can involve a lot of trial and error. Windowed envelopes are easiest and the addresses and letters can't get out of step.

- Will you use pre-printed letterhead paper, a letterhead template or just plain paper?

- Do you have a scanned version of the signature you want to use?

  It's worth making one so you don't have to sign the letters individually by hand. The procedure depends on your scanner — look at its instructions.

- What do you want the letter to say?

11.1 Making the address list

Click 🌐, go to *Documents* and open *People* (the Excel spreadsheet you made in Chapter 8).

Click the *File* tab and click 📊 Save As . The *Save As...* dialogue box opens. In *Save as type*, select *CSV (Comma delimited).* Click `Save` . You may need to click `OK` to save the active sheet and `Yes` to confirm that you don't mind omitting the formatting and charts. The address list is saved in *Documents* as *People.csv*. Close the *People* spreadsheet, discarding any changes.

> *Almost all database programs can export CSV (**Comma-Separated-Values**) files although how to do that is outside the scope of this book. As you'll see later, you can get the addresses directly from the spreadsheet or from an Access database but now that the addresses are in a CSV file, you can use the same procedure wherever they came from.*

> *If you're interested, go to Documents, right-click on People.csv, choose Open with and click Choose Program.... A list of installed programs appears. Click on Notepad to choose it and click* `OK` *. The file opens in the Notepad program: it's as if the list was on paper tape and you'd printed it. You'll see how simple it is. Data for the columns is separated with commas. The first line gives the column headings.*

> *You can't just click on People.csv to view it: the csv extension is probably associated with Excel, not Notepad (Section 5.2).*

> *If you have a CSV file from another source such as a database, you can start the procedure with the next section.*

What you learned:

- **How to export the addresses in the Excel spreadsheet as a CSV file.**
- *What a CSV (Comma-Separated-Values) file is.*
- *That addresses in other databases can be exported as a CSV file too.*
- *How to open a file with a program other than the one it's associated with.*
- *How to view a simple text file using Notepad.*
- *That you can import addresses in a spreadsheet directly.*

11.2 Making a template letter

Start a new Word document or open your letterhead template.

Click ⬚ Start Mail Merge ▾ (*Mailings/Start Mail Merge*) and click ⬚ Step by Step Mail Merge Wizard... in the box that appears. The **Mail Merge wizard** starts in a task pane to the right of the document.

> *A **Wizard** guides you through some complicated procedure.*

Check that the *Letters* radio button is selected. At the bottom of the pane, click ➡ Next: Starting document.

Check that the *Use the current document* radio button is selected. At the bottom of the pane, click ➡ Next: Select recipients.

Check that the *Use an existing list* radio button is selected. In the middle of the pane, click ⬚ Browse.... The *Select Data Source* box opens.

Click *Documents* under *Libraries* on the left side of the box. Find *People.csv* (its *Type* shows as *Microsoft Excel Comma Separated Values File*) and double-click on it.

> *You could have clicked once on the file name to select it, then clicked ⬚ Open ▾ but in many situations, including this one, you can save time by double-clicking on the file or option you want in a dialogue box.*

> *You may notice that the People.xls spreadsheet is shown too (its Type is Microsoft Excel Worksheet). When the data is in a spreadsheet, you can select that and use it directly. You can also get the data directly from some types of database (e.g. Access) but using a CSV file will almost always work.*

The *Mail Merge Recipients* box opens showing a list of the names in the file. Click ⬚ OK, then click ➡ Next: Write your letter at the bottom of the task pane.

> *We'll be using the Mail Merge Recipients box in Section 11.3.*

Tick *Ruler* (*View/Show*). Press RETURN until the text cursor is about 5.5 cm (2.2 inches) from the top of the page.

> *This distance might not be right for the envelopes you'll use. You can measure the position of the window or measure the position of the address on an existing letter that fits correctly and use those measurements instead.*

Click 📄 Address block... in the middle of the task pane. The *Insert Address Block* dialogue box opens. Click [Match Fields...].

Word expects to find particular information in the address list such as the recipients' first and last names. It's quite smart at guessing which fields in the list to use but it doesn't always get it right. In this case, you'll probably see that it hasn't managed to identify which field contains the City name. Click ▼ next to *(not matched)* alongside *City* and choose *Town* from the list that appears. Check that the other fields are matched correctly.

> *You'll see that other information such as State also shows (not matched). That's OK, the information isn't in our list anyway.*

Click [OK]. Review the other options in the *Insert Address Block* box. They're reasonably self-explanatory. When you're happy with them, click [OK].

> *Word uses Mr. Randall as an example, he's not in our address list.*

<<AddressBlock>> appears as a marker in the document showing where the address will be. Press RETURN several times, then click 📅 Date & Time *(Insert/Text)*. The Date and Time dialogue box opens. Click on the format you want to use for the date of the letter so it's highlighted. Click to tick the *Update automatically* tickbox, then click [OK].

> *Today's date appears in the document. Because you ticked Update automatically, this will automatically change to the date when you actually print the letters.*
>
> *You can use 📅 Date & Time whenever you want to put the current date in a document. Often you won't want to tick Update automatically. For example, if you write a letter to someone and keep a copy on your computer, you'll want the date to always match that on the letter that you printed and sent off.*

Press RETURN twice. Click 📄 Greeting line... in the middle of the task pane. The *Greeting Line* dialogue box opens. It's also reasonably self-explanatory. Choose the form you want for the name (e.g. *Mr. Randall*) and click [OK].

Press RETURN several times. Type *Yours sincerely* and press RETURN.

If you have a scanned signature, click ![Picture icon] Picture (*Insert/Illustrations*) and choose its file. Click on the inserted signature and drag its handles to make it the right size. You may want to type your name on another line below it.

If you don't have a scanned signature, put enough blank lines below *Yours sincerely* to make room for your signature, then type your name.

At the bottom of the task pane, click ➡ Next: Preview your letters. You see the letter with *<<AddressBlock>>* and *<<GreetingLine>>* replaced with the details for one of the names in the list filled in. Check that the letter looks OK.

> *You can step through the names in the list by clicking* [>] *and* [<] *near the top of the task pane.*

Click the *File* tab and print one of the letters. Fold the letter and try it in a windowed envelope (if you're planning to use them). Confirm that the complete address shows in the window, that the date line is comfortably below the window and that the signature spacing is OK. If there are problems, add or delete blank lines and/or change the left margin, then print and recheck the letter.

> *You can reduce the spacing between the address block lines by selecting them and clicking the No Spacing style in the styles box (Home/Styles).*

Click the *File* tab and click ![Save As icon] Save As. Choose *Word Template* as the type and type a suitable name (e.g. *FormLetter*) as the File name. Click [Save], then close Word.

> *For a one-off letter, you can work through the wizard from start to end but it's handy to have a template with the signature set up and the address block and date in the right places.*

What you learned:

- **How to start the Mail Merge wizard.**
- **How to specify the address list to be used.**
- **How to insert the address block and line it up with the envelope window.**
- **How to match fields so that the addresses are shown correctly.**
- **How to insert the date into your document and change its format.**

- **How to insert the greeting line into your letter.**
- **How to include your signature in the letter so you don't have to sign every copy.**
- *What a Wizard is.*
- *That you can often save time by double-clicking a file name or other option in a dialogue box.*
- *That you can have an inserted date stay fixed or have it update automatically.*

11.3 Sending a form letter

Click 🌀, go to *Documents* and open *FormLetter* (the template you made in Section 11.2). You may see messages that SQL commands will run. Click [Yes].

> *Word re-reads the file containing the address list. If the file containing the list has changed, the changes will be present in the new letter. If you used a CSV file, you or the database administrator will need to export it again and you'll need to reopen the template so that the letter reflects any recent changes to the database.*

Click 📄 **Start Mail Merge ▾** (*Mailings/Start Mail Merge*) and click 🖾 Step by Step Mail Merge Wizard... in the box that appears. The Mail Merge wizard restarts and the task pane appears.

At the bottom of the pane, check which step is showing. Click ➡ Next: or ⬅ Previous: if necessary to reach *Step 3* of the wizard.

> *You specified the address list file and matched the fields when you created the template. This information was stored in the template file but you can change it now if you need to use a different list. In the middle of the task pane, click on*
> 🔳 Select a different list... *and choose the list file as before.*

In the middle of the task pane, click on 🖾 Edit recipient list.... The *Mail Merge Recipients* box opens, showing all the names in the list. There's a tick box next to each name.

There might be some blank entries in the list. Click ▼ next to the Surname heading and click on *(Nonblanks)* to exclude them.

We don't want to send the letter to everyone in the list. We're going to omit anyone 65 or older or with a BMI of 30 or more. There are two ways we can do this.

The first way is simple to understand. Click ☑ to the left of *Surname* once or twice so that all the names are ticked. Scroll to the right to see the *Age* column. Click on its heading so that the names are sorted by age in increasing order.

Find the first line where the age is 65 or more and click on it so it's highlighted. Scroll to the left. Clear the tickbox on the highlighted line and on each line lower down.

Scroll to the right to see the *BMI* column. Click on its heading so that the names are sorted by BMI in increasing order.

Find the first line where the BMI is 30 or more and click on it so it's highlighted. Scroll to the left. Clear any tickboxes that are still ticked on the highlighted line and lines lower down. Only four names should still be ticked. These people would get the letter.

Now we'll try the second method which is much quicker and easier if there are hundreds of names in the list. Click ☑ to the left of *Surname* once or twice so that all the names are ticked again.

Click 🔽 Filter... . The **Query Options** dialogue box opens.

Click on the *Filter Records* tab. In the first row, choose *Age* from the *Field* drop-down list, choose *Less than* from the *Comparison:* list and enter *65* in the *Compare to:* box.

> *If you clicked (Nonblanks) earlier, this condition will already be set in the first row. Make sure the first box of the second row says And, then enter Age, Less than and 65 in that row.*

In the next row, make sure the first box says *And*. Choose *BMI* as the *Field* name and *Less than* as the *Comparison*. Enter *30* in the *Compare to:* box. Click OK . Now, you only see the same four names that were ticked before.

> *To remove a filter so all the names reappear, open the Query Options dialogue box, click Clear All then click OK .*

> *If you want the letters to be printed in a particular order, e.g. sorted by postcode, either click on the column heading or use the Sort Records tab in the Query Options box.*

> *Sorting by postcode may not work correctly: Word still has bugs.*

Of course you can manually tick or untick names in the list.

Click [OK] to close the Mail Merge Recipients box. At the bottom of the task pane, click ➡ Next: Write your letter.

> *If Word crashes at this point, restart it, click the File tab, and click* ▣ Options. *A dialogue box opens. Click Add-Ins on the left side, select COM Add-ins at the bottom and click GO.... If you see Google Desktop Office Addin in the next dialogue box, make sure it isn't ticked (it has a bug), then click* [OK]. *Try opening FormLetter and setting up the recipients again.*

If you changed the address list file from the one in the template, you need to review the field matching again. Click ▦ More items... in the middle of the task pane. The *Insert Merge Field* dialogue box opens. Click [Match Fields...], adjust the field matching as before and click [OK]. Click [Cancel] to close the Insert Merge Field box.

In the document, click below *<<GreetingLine>>* and type (pressing RETURN when you see ¶):

> *Now that you're years old, perhaps you're thinking about life insur-ance.¶*
> *I can offer you a choice of excellent policies. Please give me a call.*

Click before *years* and click ▦ More items... in the task pane. The *Insert Merge Field* dialogue box opens. Make sure the *Database Fields* radio button is selected. Double-click on *Age* in the Fields: list. Click [Close] to close the dialogue box.

Make sure there's a space before and after *<<Age>>* in the letter. Adjust the rest of the letter so it looks nice.

«AddressBlock»

Friday, 02 December 2011

«GreetingLine»

Now that you're «Age» years old, perhaps you're thinking about life insurance.

I can offer you a choice of excellent policies. Please give me a call.

Yours sincerely

John Smith

At the bottom of the task pane, click ➡ Next: Preview your letters. As when you made the letter template in Section 11.2, you can check that the letters look correct. You'll see that each person's age is shown. Click ➡ Next: Complete the merge at the bottom of the task pane.

You now have two choices. You can click on 🖳 Print... in the middle of the task pane and print the letters right away. Make sure the radio button next to *All* is selected in the first dialogue box and click ⬚ OK ⬚. Choose the printer and options in the next dialogue box and click ⬚ OK ⬚.

Alternatively, you can click 🖳 Edit individual letters... in the middle of the task pane. Make sure the radio button next to *All* is selected in the dialogue box and click ⬚ OK ⬚. Word creates a new document containing all the letters, each one starting on a new page. You can check the letters and make changes to personalise individual ones before printing the whole document as in Section 4.14.

Save the form letter document (e.g. *Document1*) if you think you might want to use it (not just the template) again. If you clicked 🖳 Edit individual letters... and personalised some of the letters, you may want to save that document (e.g. *Letters1*) too before clicking the File tab and clicking 🗀 Close.

If you're using window envelopes, you can close Word now.

If you're using address labels or printing the addresses on envelopes, click ◄ Previous: at the bottom of the task pane until you reach *Step 1* of the wizard. Continue as described in Section 11.4 for envelopes or 11.5 for labels.

> *If you're not using a scanned signature, remember to sign the letters. If you're not using window envelopes, be sure to put the letters in the right envelopes.*

What you learned:

- **How to make a new form letter using the template.**
- **That you can select a different address list.**
- **How to match fields if you're using a different list.**
- **Two ways to select recipients so only those meeting certain criteria get the letter.**
- **How to insert fields from the address list into the body of the letter itself.**
- **How to print the form letters directly to the printer.**
- **How to put the letters in a new document where you can review and personalise them before printing.**
- *That, if the database was created directly from a spreadsheet, it will stay up to date.*
- *That, if the database was created from a CSV file, the file should be updated.*
- *How to print the letters in a particular order.*
- *How to manually choose who is to receive the letter.*
- *How to remove a filter.*

11.4 Printing Envelopes

With your form letter document open and the Mail Merge task pane at *Step 1*, click to select the *Envelopes* radio button. Click ➡ Next: Starting document at the bottom of the pane.

Make sure the *Change document layout* radio button is checked and click on ▣ Envelope options... in the middle of the task pane. A dialogue box opens.

Click on the *Envelope Options* tab and choose your envelope size from the drop down list. Click on the *Printing Options* tab and click on the picture showing how you'll feed envelopes into the printer. Be sure to select whether the envelopes are fed face up or face down and whether they will be fed individually *(SSF – Single Sheet Feed)* or from a paper tray. Click [OK] and [OK] again in the confirmation box that appears.

The form letter itself is deleted and replaced with a blank page the size of the envelope. At the bottom of the task pane, click ➡ Next: Select recipients, then click ➡ Next: Arrange your envelope.

> *The envelopes need to match the letters you printed earlier. You don't want to make any changes to the recipient list or its sort order.*

If you want a return address on the envelopes, type it now, being sure to press RETURN afterwards.

In the middle of the task pane, click on ▤ Address block.... *The Insert Address Block* box appears. Check its options, then click [OK]. *<<AddressBlock>>* is added to the blank envelope. Place the text cursor before it, adjust the left margin and press RETURN repeatedly until the block is at a suitable position on the envelope.

At the bottom of the task pane, click ➡ Next: Preview your envelopes. As with the letters, you can check the envelopes. Make any needed changes to the fonts, line spacing and address block position, then click ➡ Next: Complete the merge at the bottom of the pane.

Click 🖨 Print... in the middle of the pane, choose *All* and set the print options. You may need to load the envelopes into the printer paper tray before printing or feed them individually while printing.

> *As with the letters, you can choose to create a new document containing all the envelopes but this isn't likely to be useful.*

> *Take care to stack the letters and the envelopes in the order they are printed. This makes it much easier to match them up.*

Close the document, being sure to discard the changes. You don't want to overwrite the letters themselves.

You can save a template for envelopes but it might not be much use. You'd need to be very careful to choose the right recipient list and set up the filter and sort order to match a new letter.

11.5 Printing Labels

With your form letter document open and the Mail Merge task pane at *Step 1*, click to select the *Labels* radio button. Click ➡ Next: Starting document at the bottom of the pane.

Make sure the *Change document layout* radio button is checked and click on ▤ Label options... in the middle of the task pane. A dialogue box opens.

Click on the radio button for your printer type: *Continuous-feed printers* (tractor fed labels, e.g. for a dot matrix printer) or *Page printers* (sheet fed labels – the commonest type). For a page printer, select whether the sheets are fed individually (*SSF – Single Sheet Feed*) or from a paper tray.

Word knows the dimensions for many commercial labels. Choose the label manufacturer and click to highlight the label type.

If your labels aren't listed, you can click ⌐New Label...⌐ *and enter the dimensions. These may need trial and error.*

Click ⌐ OK ⌐ and ⌐ OK ⌐ again in the confirmation box that appears. The form letter itself is deleted and replaced with a page of blank labels. At the bottom of the task pane, click ➡ Next: Select recipients, then click ➡ Next: Arrange your labels.

The labels need to match the letters you printed earlier. You don't want to make any changes to the recipient list or its sort order.

In the middle of the task pane, click on ▤ Address block.... The Insert Address Block box appears. Check its options, then click ⌐ OK ⌐. <<*AddressBlock*>> is added to the first blank label. Place the text cursor before it and adjust the left margin so that the block is at a suitable position on the label.

At the bottom of the task pane, click ➡ Next: Preview your labels. As with the letters, you can check the first label on the sheet. Make any needed changes to the margin, line spacing and font, then click ◀ Previous: Arrange your labels at the bottom of the pane.

Click [Update all labels] on the task pane. The remaining blank labels on the sheet are filled in.

With form letters and envelopes, a copy of the document is printed for each recipient. Labels are different: each page contains multiple labels. <<Next Record>> tells Word to progress to the next recipient in the list.

Click ➡ Next: Preview your labels at the bottom of the task pane. Check that the labels look correct.

Click ➡ Next: Complete the merge at the bottom of the pane.

Click 📇 Print... in the middle of the pane, choose *All* and set the print options. You may need to load the label sheets into the printer paper tray before printing or feed them individually while printing.

As with the letters, you can choose to create a new document containing all the labels but this isn't likely to be useful.

Take care to stack the letters and the sheets of labels in the order they are printed. This makes it much easier to match them up.

Close the document, being sure to discard the changes. You don't want to overwrite the letters themselves.

You can save a template for labels but it might not be much use. You'd need to be very careful to choose the right recipient list and set up the filter and sort order to match a new letter.

12 Epilogue

I hope you've found this book to be clear, informative, useful and not too overwhelming or intimidating.

Next time you need to do something, you may remember that Microsoft Office can do it but not remember how. Check the index.

There are many features of Word that the book hasn't covered. For example, you might want to format some paragraphs with a *drop capital* – a large letter at the start. Help shows how to do that.

There are many more features of Excel spreadsheet left for you to discover too.

Although web browsing is only covered very briefly and e-mail not at all, you'll have picked up enough conventions and jargon to have a good chance of figuring these out yourself.

Sometimes you'll think *Wouldn't it be useful if Windows / Word / Excel / the computer could do such and such?* It probably can. Try the Help menu or a search engine.

Of course the computer's not magic - it's not going to write a best-selling novel for you. Remember that the most important thing about anything you write isn't what it looks like. **It's what it says.**

> *Just type and type, leaving all the formatting until you're happy with what you've written.*

> *Could the order be improved? Don't retype, use cut and paste.*

> *Make full use of features such as paragraph styles, cross-references, automatic numbering and table of contents.*

> *You'll be much more willing to make changes when Word can renumber everything and you haven't invested too much time faffing about choosing fonts, etc. Leave all that to the end.*

> *You can't do that with a typewriter: that's the beauty of a word processor.*

Alphabetical Index

www.ingramcontent.com/pod-product-compliance
Lightning Source LLC
Chambersburg PA
CBHW051243050326
40689CB00007B/1043